6-minute
showstoppers

For anyone who thinks they don't have time to bake . . .

6-minute showstoppers

Delicious bakes, cakes, treats and sweets – in a flash!

sarah rainey

MICHAEL JOSEPH
an imprint of
PENGUIN BOOKS

contents

introduction

What can you do in six minutes? Drink a cup of tea . . . reply to an email . . . devour a chapter of a book . . . hang up the laundry . . . run a mile (really fast) . . .

But what if I told you that you could bake an entire cake from scratch? Make a batch of biscuits, golden and crisp from the oven? Whip up a showstopping dessert to wow guests at a dinner party? And all in about the time it takes to boil an egg.

You'd probably think I was mad. I wouldn't blame you. And before I started diving down the rabbit hole of six-minute showstoppers, I would have agreed. Six minutes might not sound like long – and trust me, I've timed it a lot lately – but it's just enough time to open up a world of delicious possibilities, if you know how.

So here's what brought me to this point. Life is short. Way too short, sometimes. And there's never enough of it to do everything we want. Baking – like learning an instrument, taking up a new sport or catching up with old friends – tends to fall by the wayside, no matter how hard we try. In the chaos of everyday life – even your average, nine-to-five, juggling-housework-with-life-admin-and-socializing-and-staying-healthy-and-remembering-to-phone-your-parents life – there simply isn't time to stop, fling on an apron and chuck a few ingredients in a bowl.

But baking isn't just a hobby. It's the ultimate 'you' time. Few things compare to the satisfaction of making a mouth-watering cake and serving it to your loved ones. Or taking time out to make a decadent dessert one evening – just for you, just because. These rituals don't simply feed our bodies. They feed the soul. At least that's how I see it.

By sacrificing baking because it takes too long or feels like too much faff, we're giving up all that. The soothing, satisfying, age-old wonder of taking raw ingredients and turning them into something tasty. And this, to me, feels like a real shame. Even as a proper keen-bean baker, I've lost count of the number of times I've taken a shop-bought sponge to a friend's house, or tucked into a packet of supermarket biscuits . . . all because I don't have the time, or energy, to make them myself.

So six-minute showstoppers are my antidote. And I hope they will become yours, too. Created for time-short, shortcut-loving home cooks, mums, dads, kids, students, busy people, impatient foodies – and everyone in between – who want to conjure up something tasty and impressive without spending all day in the kitchen. Proof, I hope, for the doubters, that baking doesn't have to be time-consuming, stressful or expensive. Instead, it can be simple, speedy and stunning.

In the pages that follow, I bring you my very favourite and fastest showstopping desserts, sweets, treats and savoury snacks. From microwave brownies to ice cream made in a freezer bag, from cheats' crème brûlées and done-in-a-flash doughnuts to cookies you can bake in a griddle pan, top-speed truffles, and biscuits that keep on cooking once you've switched the oven off.

After my first book, *Three Ingredient Baking*, came out in 2018, lots of lovely readers who got in touch said the same thing: they wanted more 'ad break' bakes – the type of thing you can rustle up in the breaks in your favourite TV show, without any proving, resting, kneading or general waiting around. So I listened, as best I could. Not only is this book packed full of quick-fire recipes, but most of them are pretty hands-off, so you can multitask to your heart's content. Guests dropped round unexpectedly? Chances are you've got the ingredients in the cupboard to make one of these while the kettle boils.

There's an instant fruity sorbet, chocolate cookies that bake in just four minutes, pizza made in a pan, pimped-up popcorn, unicorn bark, the fluffiest pancakes you'll ever taste – and countless other scrumptious treats to make you go, 'Wow!' Some are dairy-free, gluten-free and even sugar-free, while others are jam-packed with all the naughty things we're only supposed to eat in moderation.

I've tested (and eaten, in vast quantities) every single one of them – and I promise you two things . . .

Firstly, they're all showstoppers. The clue is in the name (thanks, *Bake Off*). I've designed each and every one of these recipes to impress, and – if you do them right – the results should look far more complicated and time-consuming than they really are. Whether you're feeding five people, fifty people or planning a showstopping solo meal, this book will help you go all out to make your handiwork look – and taste – really good.

Secondly, they all take six minutes to make (with one or two swifter exceptions). Six. It's not a magic number, it just happened to start with the same letter as 'showstopper'. Maybe you don't need to know that. But I was determined to better all the many brilliant books already out there which are designed for super-fast food. And six minutes just felt right.

Now don't get me wrong, I love slow cooking. Risotto, stew, bread . . . they all have a special place in my heart. But there's also a time and a place for six-minute bakes. When devising these recipes, the most important thing for me was to be realistic. Some of the recipes are ambitious and will require a bit of ambidextrous utensil work, while others are more straightforward. I'll leave you to decide which ones suit your style of baking. As well as the timing, I've tried to limit the number of steps and dishes used, so hopefully your kitchen won't look like a bomb's hit it by the end.

Perhaps counter-intuitively, the idea is not to time yourself. Sure, you can set a *Ready, Steady, Cook*-style challenge and race your friends, if that's what floats your boat. If you do, I stick by the six-minute guarantee. But, at least the first time you make these dishes, there's no need to rush.

Read right through to the end of the recipe – some of them require a bit of additional chilling or freezing or time in a cooling oven, others can be eaten straight away – and follow the 'prep' steps to the letter, weighing your ingredients out, maybe chopping or peeling, preheating whatever's needed and making sure you've got the right utensils to hand. A note here: it's the methods that take six minutes, not prepping your ingredients and kit, so it really is vital to read ahead so you know what's what. Next time around, you can do it faster. And the time after that, you can probably do it with your eyes closed.

At first glance, some of these recipes may read more like chemistry experiments than cooking instructions. You'll find yourself frying, sautéing, steaming, stirring, grilling, heating, creaming, beating, whisking and mixing, but also drizzling, squeezing, flipping, shaking and even setting one dish on fire. You see, this isn't just another boring baking book.

The many hacks and workarounds will help you learn how to 'bake' without baking at all, what happens when you deep-fry puff pastry, how to make a mousse out of marshmallows and why you need to befriend your microwave (in fact, there's a whole chapter on that). I hope it'll help you put the fun – and a little bit of magic – back into baking. Because that's what it's all about.

There's a page of thanks at the end, but for now I need to express a massive debt of gratitude to all the brilliant cookbook writers, food bloggers, YouTubers, Instagrammers, TV chefs, and of course my family and friends, for firing up my creativity and giving me so many ideas I reckon there's enough for a Volume 2. As ever, any flashes of genius in here I dedicate to you; the mistakes, bloopers and general incompetence are mine alone.

Before we get to the good stuff, I'll leave you with one final thought. Forget the timing, forget the fact that you're creating a showstopper. The whole point of this book is to encourage you to bake – using whatever time you've got – and to enjoy yourself in the process. So dig your hands in, get your fingers sticky and your apron messy, try new things – and do it all with a big smile on your face.

You're all showstoppers, in my eyes. Ready, set, bake!

Sarah Rainey
May 2020

speedy baking kit

If you're a new or novice baker, the last thing I want is for you to have to run out and buy a pile of new kit. So I've tried to keep the tins, dishes and utensils required for this book to a minimum – and they're all the sorts of things you can pick up for a bargain price at supermarkets or cookery shops.

Before you start a recipe, make sure you read the 'prep' stage – I've listed anything particular you'll need here, and the rest is general kitchenware, like bowls, spoons and plates. As these dishes are showstoppers, it's especially important to figure out how you're going to serve them – whether it's a set of ramekins or a trifle bowl – before getting stuck in.

Below, I've listed every tool, appliance and bit of gadgetry you might need to take on the recipes in this book, with stars marking the essentials. If you don't have the exact size or shape listed below, don't be put off. You can use sheets of folded tin foil to make baking trays smaller, halve or double the ingredients as required and adapt sauces or garnishes if you don't have the right utensils to hand.

A few of the microwave dishes are a little more specific, but you can easily track these down online (Silicone Worx and Ipow-Official are the best-value brands I've found) or in cookshops. Happy baking!

CAKE & LOAF TINS

- Small round cake tin (20cm diameter) *
- Standard loaf tin (1-litre capacity) *
- 12-hole muffin tray *

MICROWAVE BAKING KIT

- Round silicone cake tin (20cm diameter) *
- Square silicone baking tray (20cm x 20cm) *
- Large rectangular Pyrex dish (20cm x 30cm) *
- Heatproof plates
- Pyrex bowls, various sizes (1-litre and 1.5-litre ones are especially useful) *
- Chunky heatproof mugs (approx. 300ml capacity) *
- Silicone muffin cases (at least 8) *
- Silicone cupcake cases (at least 8)
- Silicone friand moulds (at least 8; these usually come as part of an assorted pack)

BAKING TRAYS AND DISHES

- Large rectangular baking tray (20cm x 30cm, 5cm deep) *
- Small rectangular baking tray (20cm x 25cm, 5cm deep)
- Small square baking tray (20cm x 20cm, 5cm deep)
- Several large flat metal baking sheets *

SAUCEPANS & FRYING PANS

- Large frying pan *
- Medium saucepan *
- Small saucepan
- Griddle pan
- Small iron skillet pan (20cm diameter)
- Spatter guard *

SERVING DISHES

- Set of at least 4 ramekins (8–10cm across, 6cm deep) *
- Transparent tumblers or glasses (160–300ml capacity, at least 4) *
- Large round pie or flan dish (25cm diameter) *
- Large trifle dish (mine is 3 litres but smaller is fine)
- Champagne saucers
- Large serving bowl (enough for 4 people) *
- Large serving platter
- Cupcake and petit four cases

ELECTRICAL EQUIPMENT

- Food processor, blender or hand (stick) blender (one will suffice) *
- Electric whisk
- Electronic scales

UTENSILS

- Wooden spoon *
- Rolling pin *
- Hand whisk *
- Spatula *
- Fish slice *
- Sieve *
- Scissors *
- Grater *
- Slotted spoon *
- Large chopping board *
- Palette knife
- Ladle
- Round pastry cutters (approx. 6cm and 8cm diameter)
- Fluted pasta cutter
- Pastry brush or paintbrush
- Potato peeler
- Pestle and mortar
- Ice-cream scoop

OTHER BITS & BOBS

- Mixing bowls, various sizes *
- Measuring jug *
- Piping bag and nozzles
- Lots and lots of airtight storage tins *
- Freezer-proof Tupperware containers (1-litre capacity) *
- Plastic lolly moulds (set of 4 or 6) and lids/sticks *
- Greaseproof paper *
- Tin foil *
- Ziplock freezer bags (large and small) *
- Cling film
- Kitchen paper
- String or elastic bands
- Wooden skewers
- Cocktail sticks
- Paper cups
- Matches/long-handled lighter

microwave info

I'd like to take a moment of your time to talk microwaves. You'll notice that this trusty appliance appears many times in the pages that follow. And when you're trying to bake a cake from scratch in six minutes, it'll probably become the most-used item in your kitchen.

Before cooking up these recipes, I thought I knew how to use my microwave: simply pop something inside, twizzle the dial and wait for the 'ping'. But it turns out they're actually a bit more complicated – and cleverer – than that.

So, to help you on your way to six-minute success, here are some things I've learned along the way. If you're already a micro-pro, feel free to skip to the next section.

- A quick history/science lesson. Microwave ovens came into our homes in the 1970s, revolutionizing domestic cooking and bringing the joys of convenience food into our lives. They work by transforming electrical energy into heat and channelling this directly into the molecules of the food. A generator called a magnetron takes electricity from the mains and converts it into high-powered radio waves, which are blasted into the food spinning on the turntable. The waves vibrate inside the food, causing it to heat up quickly. By contrast, a conventional oven conducts heat from the outside in. Microwaves are rarely used for baking because they don't have the browning capacity of an oven or grill – but they're powerful beasts, more than capable of creating showstoppers of their own.

- If you're thinking of buying a new microwave, make sure the door is transparent – and not reflective. So many swanky modern machines have mirrored doors, which look great on a kitchen worktop but make it really difficult to see the food inside. When you're using a microwave for baking (or even melting butter or chocolate), you really need to keep an eye on it. Being able to see what's going on can make the difference between a perfectly risen sponge and a burnt one.

- Size matters. As with most aspects of baking – the size of your cake tin, the proportions of your baking sheet or how big your eggs are – the dimensions of your microwave are pretty important. I have a retro Daewoo model (not a plug, I promise, but it's never let me down) with a 23-litre capacity. But they come in all shapes and sizes, from 13-litre ones up to 42-litre whoppers. I'd recommend using one with a capacity of at least 20 litres.

- Another note on size: you'll need a decent-sized turntable. Mine has a 28cm diameter, which means it can accommodate most dinner plates. But beware: some microwaves may look big on the outside but have tiny turntables (25cm or less), meaning you can't even fit a plate flat in there, let alone a cake tin or pie dish. The key thing is that your container can rotate, unhindered, as it cooks – or the stuff inside won't heat evenly. Square or rectangular dishes are the ones to watch, as the corners can bash on the sides of the microwave.

- Most of my recipes call for ingredients to be heated/baked/melted on the highest setting. The exact temperature depends on what category of microwave you have: a letter from A to E, usually printed on the bottom right or back of the machine. The further on in the alphabet the letter is, the higher the power – so while category-A microwaves are rare, category B means it has around 650 watts of power, category C has 700 watts, category D 750 watts and E between 800 and 850 watts. The higher the wattage, the faster your food will cook. I have a category-E microwave, so if yours is lower you may need to cook the dish for a little longer – even if you're doing so on 'high'.

- Just like ovens, microwaves tend to be temperamental – and strangely unique. Expert testers reckon there's a 5–10 per cent difference in heating power and timing even between microwaves of the same category. So get to know yours. Use it frequently. Talk to it (not really). Try baking different things in there and watch them closely to see how your microwave behaves. You'll soon learn if it needs 20 seconds longer or 20 seconds less than average.

- Not content with simply being a microwave, some modern-day appliances are 'convection ovens' too, meaning they combine the traditional cooking techniques of a conventional oven with the inside-out methods of a microwave – all in one box. None of the recipes here require you to have a convection oven, but it's not a problem if you do, as you can use just the micro function. You can also ignore the extraneous settings for defrosting meat, steaming veg and poaching fish, etc., which will be eternally confusing to us all.

- Don't forget that there are certain materials you should never put inside a microwave. Namely metal. And that means tin foil, cookware with a metal (gold, silver or copper) trim and stainless steel crockery or cutlery. Other things that fare badly are paper bags, takeaway containers and yoghurt or butter pots, which tend to be made of the sort of plastic that melts under intense heat. Certain foods are also no-gos: grapes (which can explode) and hot peppers (which release chemicals that burn your eyes when heated). If you're melting butter or cooking with oil, place a sheet of kitchen paper over the top of the dish to stop grease spattering everywhere. And always check that mugs, bowls and plates are microwave-safe before putting them in there; some ceramics get extremely hot and may burn your hands. I've found the best material is silicone, which is flexible and heat-resistant up to 300°C – and you can get all sorts of nifty silicone bakeware (from cake and loaf tins to muffin cases) online. See the 'Speedy Baking Kit' section for my must-have items.

- Finally . . . the big question: is all this microwaving bad for you? I remember once being warned to stay away from the glass door in case I was 'microwaved', and certainly never to lean or put anything on top of the microwave as it would be exposed to dangerous radiation. The internet is awash with claims that microwaves can cause everything from cataracts to cancer and zap all the nutrients from your food. There's no evidence for any of this, so you needn't worry about it cooking you rather than those showstoppers.

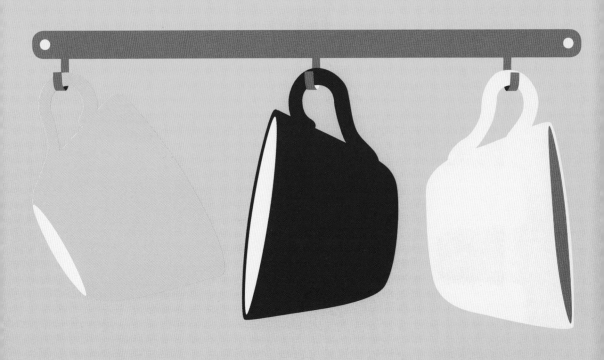

CHAPTER 1:

microwave cakes

Whether it's a mug cake for one or a decadent sponge
to mark a special occasion, these cakes are all conjured
up with a little bit of microwave magic

Peanut butter and jam brownies ◇ Choca-mocha cake
◇ Gin and tonic lemon drizzle ◇ Kit Kat cake ◇ Honey orange cake
◇ Spiced apple mug cake ◇ Cinnamon roll mug cake ◇ Molten mug cake
◇ Mince pie mug cake ◇ Red velvet mug cake

PEANUT BUTTER and JAM BROWNIES

PB and J is a classic combination . . . good on toast, delicious in a bagel, but *absolutely incredible* when you combine it with a chocolate brownie. These chocolatey treats are oh so rich and are topped with pretty swirls of peanut butter and your favourite fruit jam.

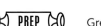 **MAKES 20**

200g caster sugar

70g cocoa powder

60g plain flour

150g unsalted butter, melted

2 eggs

1 tsp vanilla extract

75g peanut butter (I like crunchy but smooth is fine)

75g jam (again, it's up to you – I like classic raspberry best)

 PREP

Grease a small square Pyrex or silicone dish (approx. 20cm x 20cm) around the sides and base with a little butter. You'll also need a palette knife.

—

START THE CLOCK

Mix the dry brownie ingredients together before stirring in the melted butter, eggs and vanilla extract. Beat until smooth.

Transfer the batter to the prepared dish and use the palette knife to spread it to the edges and even out the top.

Dot teaspoonfuls of peanut butter and jam over the top of the brownies and use a knife to swirl them around a little.

Microwave on high for 5 minutes, checking halfway and rotating the dish if you need to (sometimes square dishes are too big to rotate inside the microwave, so this will ensure they cook evenly).

Let the brownies cool completely before slicing into squares and tucking in. They'll keep for 5 to 6 days in an airtight tin.

 TIP

—

Try swapping the peanut butter for other types of nut butter or even tahini, a Middle Eastern condiment made from toasted ground sesame seeds, which tastes great with blackberry jam.

CHOCA-MOCHA CAKE

I've never been a hardened coffee drinker, so a mocha – that moreish combination of coffee and chocolate – is my go-to hot drink. This recipe combines these two favourite flavours in a moist, fudgey cake, topped with a super-speedy coffee icing that you can drizzle on while it's still hot.

 SERVES
8–10

30g cocoa powder

3 heaped tsp instant coffee

175g self-raising flour, sifted

175g caster sugar

60ml semi-skimmed milk

60ml sunflower oil

1 egg

1 tsp vanilla extract

For the icing:

1 heaped tsp instant coffee

130g icing sugar, sifted

 PREP Grease a 20cm-round, microwave-proof cake dish with a little butter and line the base with greaseproof paper.

 START THE CLOCK Mix the cocoa powder and 3 teaspoons of coffee together in a small bowl and add approximately 100ml boiling water. Stir vigorously until dissolved.

In a separate bowl, mix together the flour and sugar. Add the coffee mixture, followed by the milk, oil, egg and vanilla extract. Beat to combine.

Pour the batter into the prepared cake dish and microwave on high for 4.5 to 5 minutes, checking throughout. You'll know it's ready when it's risen and spongey (not wet) on top.

While the cake bakes, make the icing. In a small bowl, add a splash of water to the remaining teaspoon of instant coffee and mix to make a paste.

Mix in the icing sugar, a little at a time, adding more water if you need to, until you have a smooth paste, roughly the texture of thick cream.

When the cake is done, carefully tip it out on to a cooling rack and immediately spread the icing over the top (or drizzle, if you're more artistic than me). You may want to put a plate or chopping board underneath the rack as this bit can get messy.

If you like, sprinkle chopped walnuts, pecans or coffee beans around the edge of the cake for a pretty finish – do this before the icing sets so they stick.

You can serve it hot and gooey, as a stodgy pudding with ice cream, or wait until it cools and eat a slice alongside a nice cup of tea. The cake will keep for 3 to 4 days in an airtight tin.

 TIP *A silicone cake mould (rather than Pyrex glass or unbendy plastic) tends to be best for this recipe, as it makes it easier to get the cake out without burning your hands. Just run a blunt knife around the inside edge if it's sticking.*

GIN and TONIC LEMON DRIZZLE

Gin and tonic is my tipple of choice. I also love lemon drizzle cake. So the prospect of combining the two – especially in a mug cake you can whip up in a matter of minutes – made me very excited. Not only does this little gem have a gin-infused glaze, but it's also soaked through with a gin and tonic drizzle that makes it extra-moist and delicious.

 SERVES 1

For the cake:

50g plain flour

¼ tsp baking powder

25g caster sugar

zest and juice of ½ a lemon

1 egg

1 tbsp sunflower or vegetable oil

For the drizzle:

15g caster sugar

1 tsp gin

1 tbsp tonic water

For the glaze:

40g icing sugar

1 tsp gin

 PREP

You'll need a good, chunky, microwave-proof mug (approx. 300ml), buttered lightly on the inside. And a wooden skewer will help spread the drizzle.

 START THE CLOCK

Mix all the dry ingredients (including the lemon zest) together in the mug.

Then add the lemon juice, egg, oil and mix well, until combined and smooth.

Microwave on high for 1 to 1.5 minutes (all mugs/microwaves are different, so check it after 1 minute and only give it the extra 30 seconds if it needs it. You'll know it's ready when it's risen to the top of the mug).

While the cake cooks, make the drizzle by mixing the sugar, gin and tonic together in a small bowl or ramekin. Keep stirring until the sugar dissolves. For the glaze, sieve the icing sugar into the gin and stir until smooth.

When the cake is done, poke holes with a skewer and pour the drizzle on top, making sure it seeps into the sponge. Top with the glaze and eat hot.

TIP

If you have trouble squeezing lemons, or come across one that's particularly hard, try microwaving the lemon (whole) for 20 to 30 seconds. Let it cool slightly, slice it in half – and you'll find it much easier to squeeze out all that juice.

KIT KAT CAKE

I'm a big fan of turning my favourite chocolate bars into desserts . . . and this Kit Kat cake does exactly what it says on the tin. Rather than make a chocolate sponge, I've gone for a fluffy vanilla base, studded with crumbled Kit Kats and topped with yet more chocolate wafer pieces.

 SERVES 8–10

150g plain flour

1 tsp baking powder

150g caster sugar

150g unsalted butter, melted

80ml semi-skimmed milk

3 eggs

6 Kit Kats, crumbled

 PREP

Grease a 20cm-round, microwave-proof cake dish (silicone is best) with a little butter and line the base with a circle of greaseproof paper. This will make it easier to get the cake out once it's baked. You'll also need a palette knife.

 START THE CLOCK

Sieve the flour and baking powder into a bowl, add the sugar and stir to combine. Add the melted butter and milk and crack in the eggs one by one, stirring between each.

Mix in four of the crumbled Kit Kat biscuits.

Tip the cake mix into the prepared tin and use the palette knife to smooth the top. Microwave on high for 4.5 minutes, until the cake is spongey and risen.

Once the cake is baked, immediately scatter the two remaining crumbled Kit Kats over the top – they'll melt and stick to the top of the sponge.

Leave it to cool completely in the tin before slicing. It makes the perfect afternoon pick-me-up – or, if you're saving it for a special occasion, it'll keep for 4 to 5 days in an airtight container.

 TIP

To crumble the Kit Kats, or any chocolate/biscuit, keep it in its wrapper and give it several bashes on the side of your kitchen worktop. This will break it into nice-sized chunks without the mess (although you'll have less excuse to lick your fingers afterwards).

HONEY ORANGE CAKE

With a dense, crumbly texture – a bit like polenta cake – this sponge is positively bursting with zesty orange and deliciously sweet honey. It tastes nicest hot, topped with a spoonful of crème fraîche, but can be enjoyed cold, too. You could jazz it up by using flavoured honey, such as lavender or ginger.

 SERVES 8–10

190g ground almonds

2 tsp baking powder

3 eggs

100ml fresh orange juice

2 tbsp orange marmalade, mashed with a fork so it breaks up

4 tbsp runny honey

30g flaked almonds

 PREP

Grease a large Pyrex pie or flan dish (mine is 25cm across and 1.1-litre capacity) with a little butter or oil. A shallow dish is better than a cake tin here, as you don't want the cake to be too deep.

You'll also need to preheat the grill to high and put a baking tray underneath.

 START THE CLOCK

In a large bowl, mix together all the cake ingredients (minus the flaked almonds, and using only 3 tbsp of honey) and lightly beat until smooth.

Scrape the batter into the Pyrex dish, spreading it around so it covers the base and the top is nice and even. Microwave on high for 4.5 minutes.

Meanwhile, spread the almonds out on the baking tray (be careful, it will be hot) and put them under the grill for 3 to 4 minutes. Keep an eye on them – they toast quickly.

When the cake is baked – you'll know it's ready when the sponge is dry to the touch – take it out and, placing a plate over the top of the dish, upend it on to the plate.

Sprinkle the toasted almonds over the top, then drizzle over the remaining honey and serve warm. You should notice lots of lovely honey oozing out as you slice into it – and the kitchen will be filled with gorgeous citrussy aromas.

The cake will keep for 3 to 4 days in the fridge or an airtight container.

SPICED APPLE MUG CAKE

Come autumn, when there's a glut of apples falling from the trees (or into your trolley), there's nothing better than baking them into a golden, spiced apple sponge. My mug cake captures all those rich autumnal flavours in miniature, topped with an oaty-toffee crumble.

 SERVES 1

For the cake:

50g plain flour

¼ tsp baking powder

20g soft dark brown sugar

¼ tsp each of:
ground cinnamon
mixed spice
ground nutmeg

2 tbsp apple sauce

2 tsp vegetable oil

1 small apple, peeled, cored and chopped into small chunks

For the crumble topping:

20g salted butter

20g rolled oats

20g dark brown sugar

½ tsp cinnamon

1 tbsp runny honey

 PREP

Clean and dry a large, microwave-proof mug (approx. 300ml capacity).

—

 START THE CLOCK

Put the butter for the crumble topping in the mug and microwave on high for around 20 seconds until it melts (this will also grease the mug). While it cooks, mix the other crumble ingredients together in a bowl. Then add the melted butter and stir to combine.

In a separate bowl, mix all the cake ingredients except the chopped apple. Once combined, stir in the apple chunks.

Transfer the cake mix to the mug and use the back of a spoon to flatten it slightly. Top with the crumble, pressing it down so it's all tightly packed.

Microwave on high for 3 minutes.

Let the mug cool slightly – you don't want to burn your hands on all that hot sugar – before removing from the microwave to serve. You can either eat it straight from the mug or turn it out and serve with a scoop of vanilla ice cream.

 TIP

—

Keep an eye on mug cakes when baking them in the microwave as they might cook faster or overspill depending on the size, thickness and material of your mug!

CINNAMON ROLL MUG CAKE

Sticky, stodgy dough swirled with cinnamon sugar and topped with cream cheese icing (although I always think the American 'frosting' sounds more appealing), there are few things in life better than cinnamon rolls. Use this recipe to bake one yourself . . . it's made in the microwave but it tastes like it's fresh out of a bakery oven.

 SERVES 1

For the roll:

85g plain flour

20g caster sugar

¼ tsp baking powder

¼ tsp ground cinnamon

¼ tsp ground nutmeg

1 tbsp semi-skimmed milk

2 tbsp vegetable or sunflower oil

For the swirl:

15g soft light brown sugar

½ tsp ground cinnamon

½ tbsp unsalted butter, melted

For the icing:

1 tbsp cream cheese

½ tbsp unsalted butter, melted

25g icing sugar, sifted

PREP

Clean and dry a chunky, microwaveable mug (approx. 300ml). You'll also need a small piping bag or sandwich bag, and a fork or wooden skewer for the swirl.

 START THE CLOCK

Mix all the roll ingredients together in a small bowl, starting with the dry components and then adding the milk and oil.

Put all the swirl ingredients in a ramekin and stir to combine.

Spoon half the batter into the prepared mug and swirl over half the cinnamon mixture, using a fork or a skewer to work it down into the batter. Repeat, topping with the remainder of the cinnamon swirl.

Microwave on high for 2 minutes, until the roll puffs up to the top of the mug.

While it cooks, make the icing. Use a fork to whisk everything together until smooth. Decant into the piping bag, or if using a sandwich bag, squeeze the icing to one corner and use a pair of scissors to snip off the end, creating a hole around ½ cm wide.

You can leave the cinnamon roll in the mug or tip it out before piping a swirl of icing on top. Don't worry if some drizzles down the sides – the more the better! Eat it straight away: warm, gooey and guaranteed to give you sticky fingers.

MOLTEN MUG CAKE

Quick, indulgent and unashamedly delicious, my molten mug cake hits the spot if you're craving something sweet, at any time of day or night. You can whip one up with basics from the cupboard – and my secret ingredient gives it the gooiest melting middle ever.

 SERVES 1

20g unsalted butter

35g plain flour

10g cocoa powder

35g caster sugar

½ tsp baking powder

½ tsp vanilla extract

25ml semi-skimmed milk

1 white Lindor chocolate/a couple of chunks of your favourite chocolate

 PREP

You'll need a chunky microwaveable mug (mine is just over 300ml). You can use a heatproof ramekin or small bowl if you prefer, just make sure it's at least 10cm deep.

—

 START THE CLOCK

Put the butter in the mug and microwave on high for 20 to 30 seconds until it melts.

While the butter melts, mix the dry ingredients together in a small bowl. Add the vanilla extract and milk and stir to make a paste.

Tip the paste into the mug with the melted butter and stir – I use a blunt knife rather than a fork or spoon to get rid of all the lumps – until you have a smooth mixture. Smooth out the top.

Gently press a whole (unwrapped!) Lindor or other chocolate down into the centre of the mix until it nearly disappears.

Microwave the mug cake on high for around 1 minute, checking after 50 seconds or so. It should rise to the top of the mug and then slowly sink as it cools.

Eat immediately, topped – if you want – with ice cream or whipped cream, straight from the mug.

 TIP

—

You can microwave two of these at once – just add around 30 seconds to the cooking time and keep an eye on the cakes so they don't burn. Alternatively, make the cake mixture for both, divide it between two mugs and cook one after the other.

MINCE PIE MUG CAKE

Mince pies aren't just for Christmas . . . okay, so usually they are, but I came up with this recipe after finding a packet of them in my freezer one July. A fairy-light sponge, spiced with festive flavours and filled with gooey mincemeat – all it's missing is the stodgy pastry. And there's even enough for two.

 MAKES 2

60g unsalted butter, softened

30g soft light brown sugar

60g self-raising flour

1 tsp mixed spice

10ml semi-skimmed milk

1 egg

100g shop-bought mincemeat

icing sugar, for dusting

 PREP

Grease the insides of two chunky, microwave-proof mugs (approx. 300ml each) with a little butter.

 START THE CLOCK

Cream together the butter and the sugar, before adding the flour and mixed spice.

Mix in the milk and the egg, stirring until you have a smooth, pale-coloured batter.

Put a quarter of the batter into each mug. Top with half the mincemeat and then the remainder of the batter.

Microwave them together on high for 3 minutes. You'll know the cakes are ready when the sponges rise to the top of the mugs and your kitchen is filled with the lovely smell of hot mince pies.

Dust the cakes with icing sugar before tucking in. Be careful – just like in a regular mince pie, the mincemeat in the middle gets veeeeeery hot!

RED VELVET MUG CAKE

There was a time when red velvet cake seemed to be taking over bakeries and cupcake shops all around the world. And no wonder: the fluffy cocoa sponge is utterly delicious. Tuck into this mini version on a cold winter's night, with your slippers on and something soppy and romantic on TV.

 SERVES 1

For the cake:

40g self-raising flour

50g golden caster sugar

2 tbsp cocoa powder

3 tbsp sunflower or
    vegetable oil

3 tbsp semi-skimmed milk

1 egg

½ tsp red gel food colouring

For the icing:

25g icing sugar

2 tsp cream cheese

 PREP Grease the inside of a chunky, microwave-proof mug (approx. 300ml) with a little butter or flavourless oil. You'll also need a whisk to mix the wet ingredients.

**START
THE CLOCK** Mix all the dry ingredients together until combined.

Add the oil, milk and egg and whisk well. Finally, add the food colouring, stirring as you do so you can get the colour just right. You're looking for a vivid red; remember it will fade slightly as it cooks and the cocoa colouring comes through.

Microwave on high for 1 to 1.5 minutes. Check it as it bakes – it may not need the full amount of time, but you'll know it's done when the sponge rises to the top of the mug.

While the cake cooks, make the icing. Sieve the icing sugar over the cream cheese and mix well – it should be smooth but not too runny.

Once the cake is done, spoon or pipe (if you want to be neat) the icing on top. Tuck in immediately, straight from the mug. Mmmmmm!

 TIP *I find gel food colouring better than traditional water-based colouring as it's more vivid and will give your bakes lovely vibrant hues. If you want to make this cake really showstopping, swap the cream cheese icing for a scoop of your favourite ice cream, chocolate sauce, sweets and biscuit crumbs. Et voilà! Your very own red velvet sundae.*

CHAPTER 2:

biscuits and buns

From cookies baked in a pan to mouth-watering muffins,
mini cakes and snack bars, these biscuits and buns
can all be made in an instant

Chocolate crackle cookies ◇ Honey nut yoghurt bars ◇ Welsh cakes
◇ Jammy thumbprint cookies ◇ Nutella griddle cookies ◇ Snickerdoodles
◇ Banana-coco muffins ◇ Choc chip cookie pots ◇ Flat white friands
◇ Cake crumb cookies ◇ Fluffy ricotta biscuits

CHOCOLATE CRACKLE COOKIES

These fudgey biscuits – also called 'crinkle cookies' – get their name because of the 'crackled' effect on top, which forms as the dough bakes and rises through the layer of icing sugar. Tooth-achingly sweet, they're perfect for that moment when nothing but a chocolate biscuit will do.

 MAKES 8

100g caster sugar

30g dark chocolate, melted

1 tbsp sunflower or
  vegetable oil

1 egg

½ tsp vanilla extract

65g plain flour

½ tsp baking powder

1 tbsp cocoa powder

a pinch of salt

30g icing sugar, sifted

 PREP

Preheat the oven to 250°C (fan 230°C) and line a large baking sheet with grease-proof paper.

—

 START THE CLOCK

In a large bowl, beat together the sugar, chocolate, oil, egg and vanilla extract until smooth.

Sieve the flour, baking powder, cocoa powder and salt together in another bowl. Stir to combine and then fold this into the liquid mixture.

Put the icing sugar into a separate bowl, ready for rolling the cookies.

Using a dessert spoon, drop heaped spoonfuls of the cookie dough (it will be very wet; don't worry – just prepare for messy hands) into the bowl of icing sugar, one by one. Roll them around until they're completely coated, then use a clean spoon to transfer them to the baking sheet.

Space them out as much as possible – they'll spread as they bake, so unless you want one giant crackle cookie (which isn't a bad idea), leave plenty of gaps.

Sprinkle any leftover icing sugar over the tops of the cookies, before putting on the top shelf of the oven to bake for 4 minutes.

When they're done, switch the oven off and open the door slightly. Leave the cookies inside for 15 to 20 minutes to cool. They'll start to firm up, but you want to tuck in while they're still warm and fudgey inside, so don't leave them too long.

The cookies will keep for up to 5 days in an airtight tin.

HONEY NUT YOGHURT BARS

Crunchy, crispy, salty, sweet … these are like no snack bars you've ever tasted, topped with smooth, tangy yoghurt. You can wrap them up and take them to work, have them as an afternoon energy booster – or tuck into them for breakfast (they're made from cereal and yoghurt, after all).

MAKES 16–20

100g crunchy nut cornflakes

75g whole peanuts

75g whole almonds

30g desiccated coconut

60g unsalted butter, melted

2 tbsp honey

100g crunchy peanut butter

For the topping:

1 tbsp warm water

½ tsp vanilla extract

½ tsp powdered gelatine

80g Greek yoghurt

1 tbsp runny honey

300g icing sugar, sifted

 PREP

Line a large rectangular baking tray (20cm x 30cm, at least 5cm deep) with tin foil. You'll also need a palette knife or a large spoon.

 START THE CLOCK

Pour the cornflakes into a bowl, gently crush them with a wooden spoon and stir in the nuts and coconut.

In a separate bowl, mix the melted butter with the honey and peanut butter. Tip this into the cereal mixture and stir to combine. Then, transfer the sticky mix to the prepared tray and press it down firmly, using the palette knife or the back of a spoon to ensure it's tightly compacted.

To make the topping, mix the water, vanilla extract and gelatine together in a ramekin and stir for a minute or so until it thickens. Set aside.

Put the yoghurt and honey in a microwaveable bowl and heat for 20 seconds until runny. Stir in the gelatine mixture and, once combined, the sifted icing sugar.

You should end up with a smooth, thick liquid, the consistency of double cream. Pour this on to the cornflake layer and spread it over so it covers it completely.

Transfer the tray to the fridge for at least 2 hours to allow the mixture to set. Use a sharp knife to cut into bars, and store in the fridge or an airtight container. They should keep for 4 to 5 days.

WELSH CAKES

Disclaimer: I am not Welsh. I love Wales, though, and Welsh people . . . and most of all I love Welsh cakes. This super-speedy version of the traditional griddle cakes, filled with spiced currants and covered with crunchy sugar, makes the perfect teatime treat.

 MAKES 6

120g plain flour

½ tsp baking powder

½ tsp mixed spice

60g caster sugar

50g unsalted butter, softened

1 egg, beaten

35g currants (or raisins, sultanas or dried fruit)

 PREP

Place a large frying pan over a high heat on the hob and put a knob of butter in to melt, swirling it around so it covers the base.

 START THE CLOCK

Mix the dry ingredients together, holding back 10g of the sugar for sprinkling on the Welsh cakes at the end.

Add the softened butter and work it into the mixture, using a wooden spoon to press it into the sides of the bowl. You should end up with something resembling breadcrumbs.

Stir in the beaten egg and add the dried fruit. Now it's time to roll your sleeves up and dig your hands in: bring the mixture together into a ball and knead it for a few seconds between your fingers. It should have the same texture as soft pastry dough.

Divide the mixture into six balls, rolling each in your palms.

Arrange them in the hot pan, flattening them down (you can use a fish slice if you have one, or the back of a spoon) to make six large discs, roughly 1cm thick.

Griddle on each side for 2 minutes, until they're golden brown, puffed up and firm.

Transfer the Welsh cakes to a large plate or board and sprinkle over the remaining sugar. Serve hot or cold, with butter or just as they are.

They'll keep for 4 days in an airtight container.

 TIP

Though they're coated in sugar, these taste great topped with a few slices of cheese and chutney. Brie and Cheddar are especially good – the combo of sweet and salty works a treat.

JAMMY THUMBPRINT COOKIES

These sticky, fruity cookies make me feel a bit like a five-year-old – not only when I eat them, but when I make them, too, squidging my thumb into the middle to make a hole for the jam. The short cooking time makes them nice and crumbly, rather than crisp, and the jam is deliciously gooey.

MAKES 12

250g ground almonds

1 egg

60ml coconut oil, melted

3 tbsp maple syrup

1 tsp vanilla extract

140g fruit jam of your choice

PREP

Preheat the oven to 250°C (fan 230°C) and line a baking sheet with greaseproof paper.

START THE CLOCK

Mix the almonds, egg, coconut oil, maple syrup and vanilla extract together in a bowl until they come together into a loose dough.

Roll blobs of dough (around the size of ping-pong balls) between your palms and spread them out on the baking sheet.

Flatten them with your fingers until the cookies are around 1cm thick. Then squidge your thumb into the centre of each to create a deep dent (make sure you don't make a hole all the way through or the jam will leak out).

Fill the dent in each cookie with a heaped teaspoonful of jam.

Place the baking sheet of cookies in the oven on the top shelf and cook for 4 minutes. When they're done, open the door slightly, rotate the baking sheet (to ensure the cookies don't catch or burn) and leave them to cool in the oven with the door ajar for around half an hour.

Enjoy hot or cold, with a cup of tea. The cookies will keep for 5 to 6 days in an airtight tin.

NUTELLA GRIDDLE COOKIES

Ideal for when you don't have space in the oven or simply can't be bothered with the faff of baking traditional biscuits, these griddle cookies couldn't be easier. The combination of toasty oats and smooth Nutella makes them irresistible – I challenge you not to eat at least one straight from the pan!

 MAKES 8

130g rolled oats

160g Nutella

1 egg

½ tsp baking powder

1 tbsp icing sugar

 PREP

Grease a large frying pan with a little sunflower or vegetable oil (don't use butter – it will burn) and place it over a medium heat on the hob. You'll also need a sheet of tin foil and a fish slice.

 START THE CLOCK

In a large bowl, mix the oats, Nutella, egg and baking powder together until well combined.

Wet your hands (this will stop the mixture sticking to them) and roll the cookie dough into eight small balls, roughly the size of ping-pong balls.

Arrange them in the pan and, using the back of a spoon, flatten them down slightly to make cookie-shaped discs.

Cook for 2 minutes on each side, covering the pan with tin foil to keep the heat in and carefully flipping them over with the fish slice once they're done on one side. Be gentle – the dough is very soft at this stage, and you don't want it to burn or fall apart.

When the cookies are baked on both sides, slide them out of the pan and on to a plate. Don't worry if they're still soft and crumbly, they will firm up as they cool.

Sieve the icing sugar liberally over the top. They'll keep for up to 5 days in an airtight container.

SNICKERDOODLES

These soft, buttery biscuits covered in cinnamon sugar are named after the German word for 'crinkly noodle'. The secret ingredient is cream of tartar, which makes the cookie dough rise and then fall as it cools, giving its characteristic top.

**MAKES
12**

110g unsalted butter, softened

75g caster sugar

50g light brown sugar

175g plain flour

½ tsp cream of tartar

½ tsp bicarbonate of soda

½ tsp ground cinnamon

1 egg

1 tsp vanilla extract

For rolling the cookies:

40g granulated sugar

1 tsp cinnamon

 PREP

Preheat the oven to 250°C (fan 230°C) and line a large baking sheet with greaseproof paper.

**START
THE CLOCK**

Cream the butter and sugars together and beat until fluffy and smooth.

Add the dry ingredients, followed by the egg and vanilla extract, and stir until well combined.

In a separate bowl, mix together the granulated sugar and cinnamon.

Take small handfuls of the dough and roll them between your palms to make small balls – roughly the size of ping-pong balls. Drop these in the cinnamon sugar and shake them around until they're completely coated.

Space the dough balls out on the baking sheet. Don't flatten them down, and make sure there's at least 3–4cm between them – they will spread as they cook.

Bake the cookies on the top shelf of the oven for 4 minutes. They should puff up and then start to sink as soon as you turn the heat off, and the edges should be turning golden.

Switch off the oven, leave the door ajar and let the cookies cool on the oven shelf for around half an hour. This will help them crisp up.

Eat hot or cold. I know all cookies taste good with ice cream, but these are especially wonderful. They'll stay fresh for 4 to 5 days, stored in an airtight tin.

BANANA-COCO MUFFINS

Good for breakfast, elevenses or an afternoon snack, banana muffins are a classic. These can easily be whipped up in an ad break during your favourite TV show. The cinnamon and toasty coconut gives the fluffy sponge a rich, wholesome flavour.

 MAKES 8

2 ripe bananas, peeled

100g unsalted butter, softened

1 egg

2 tbsp semi-skimmed milk

100g self-raising flour, sifted

100g soft light brown sugar

1 tsp cinnamon

50g desiccated coconut

 PREP

Preheat the grill to high. You'll need eight microwave-proof muffin cases – I use silicone ones, as they hold their shape even when the batter is raw. Just make sure you use tall muffin cases rather than smaller cupcake ones, or your muffins will overflow as they bake.

—

 START THE CLOCK

Cut eight slices from one of the bananas and mash all the rest into the softened butter. Add the egg and milk and mix well.

Add the dry ingredients, holding back 20g of the desiccated coconut, and stir until you have a thick, smooth batter.

Divide the batter between the muffin cases and top with a slice of banana. Microwave them all together, on high, for 4 minutes.

While the muffins are baking, spread the remainder of the coconut out on a baking sheet and put it under the grill for no more than 2 minutes. Keep an eye on it – it browns quickly.

Sprinkle the toasted coconut over the baked muffins and allow them to cool completely before eating.

They'll keep for 4 to 5 days in an airtight container, and taste even better warmed, with cream and a dollop of toffee sauce.

CHOC CHIP COOKIE POTS

I'm a sucker for choc chip cookies, especially the ones that are soft and crumbly, with still-melted chocolate dotted throughout the dough. In fact, I love cookie dough so much I could scoff the lot straight from the mixing bowl. These little pots combine the best of both worlds: the dough is ever so slightly under-baked, so it's still fudgey in the middle, but the tops are crumbly like a cake.

 MAKES 4

75g unsalted butter, softened	½ tsp bicarbonate of soda
55g soft light brown sugar	a pinch of salt
1 egg	100g plain flour, sifted
½ tsp vanilla extract	100g dark or milk chocolate, chopped into chunks

 PREP

You'll need four ramekins (mine are approx. 8cm in diameter and 6cm deep). Grease them with a little butter before you start.

—

 START THE CLOCK

Cream the butter and sugar together until pale and fluffy. Mix in the egg and vanilla extract.

Stir the bicarbonate of soda and salt into the flour and then add this to the butter mixture. Finally, add the chocolate chips and stir well until combined.

Divide the cookie dough between the four ramekins, using a teaspoon to flatten it down and neaten the tops.

Microwave on high for 3 minutes, watching the little pots as they puff up while they cook.

Remove them carefully (the ramekins can get hot) and serve warm, topped with scoops of ice cream.

You can store them for a day or two in the fridge and reheat before serving, but they're best eaten on the day they're made.

—

 TIP

You can use shop-bought chocolate chips for this recipe, but I'd recommend chopping up a bar of your favourite milk or dark chocolate instead. Not only is the cocoa quality higher, but it means you can keep the chunks nice and generous, so they don't get lost in the dough.

FLAT WHITE FRIANDS

A friand is a small oval or rectangular almond cake, popular in Australia and New Zealand, a sort of Down Under take on the French *financier*. My versions are inspired by my favourite coffee, characterized by its 'microbubbles' – so in honour of the flat white, these have a delicate, frothy top.

 MAKES 10

80g unsalted butter, softened

85g soft light brown sugar

2 eggs, beaten

60g ground almonds

25g self-raising flour

2 tsp cheats' espresso (made by dissolving 1 heaped tsp instant coffee in 2 tsp hot water)

20g walnut pieces, finely chopped

For the icing:

25g unsalted butter, softened

1 tbsp semi-skimmed milk

1 tsp cheats' espresso (as previously)

75g icing sugar, sifted

 PREP

Clean and dry ten microwave-proof friand moulds (mine are approx. 6cm long x 2cm wide). Any silicone cake cases will do – you can use regular cupcake cases if you don't have the right shape to hand.

 START THE CLOCK

Cream the butter and sugar together. Add the beaten eggs, followed by the rest of the ingredients, stirring as you go until everything is combined.

Divide the mixture between the ten moulds, making sure to fill them only about two-thirds full – the batter will rise as it cooks.

To make transferring easier, I take the rotating plate out of the microwave and balance the friand moulds on that, before setting it back in place. Microwave the cakes on high for 3.5 minutes.

While they bake, make the icing by combining all the ingredients with a fork or a whisk, if you have one to hand. You should end up with a smooth, thick buttercream.

Allow the friands to cool slightly before topping with frothy clouds of icing. You can spread it on liberally or pipe it if you're feeling neat.

Eat hot or cold, alongside a flat white (what else?!). They'll keep for 3 to 4 days in an airtight tin.

CAKE CRUMB COOKIES

If your family is anything like mine, leftover cake is a rare phenomenon . . . but if you do ever find yourself with some offcuts of sponge or slices of birthday cake in need of a good home, these soft, chewy cookies will give them a new lease of life. You can use any variety of cake: icing, filling and all.

MAKES 20

200g plain flour, sifted

½ tsp bicarbonate of soda

20g cocoa powder

115g unsalted butter, softened

115g caster sugar

115g dark brown sugar

1 egg

½ tsp vanilla extract

200g leftover cake, chopped into small crumbs (my favourite is gooey chocolate cake)

PREP

Preheat the oven to 250°C (fan 230°C) and line two large baking sheets with grease-proof paper.

START THE CLOCK

In a large bowl, mix together the flour, bicarbonate of soda and cocoa powder. In another, blend the butter with the sugars, egg and vanilla extract.

Combine the two and stir in the cake crumbs.

Divide the mixture into pieces, around the size of ping-pong balls. Arrange them on the two baking sheets (don't worry, they shouldn't spread) and flatten each one slightly with a fork or clean fingers.

Bake on the top shelf of the oven for 4 minutes. When they're done, leave the cookies to cool entirely in the oven with the door slightly ajar – this should take no more than half an hour.

They're best eaten on the day they're made, but they'll keep for 3 to 4 days in an airtight container if you want to bake them ahead of time.

FLUFFY RICOTTA BISCUITS

Delicately flavoured with the zing of Sicilian lemon, these fluffy ricotta biscuits have the melt-in-the-mouth consistency of sponge. They're not the prettiest biscuits in the tin, but serve them up to accompany a digestif or a creamy mousse and that won't matter one bit.

MAKES ABOUT 12

85g unsalted butter, softened

130g caster sugar

1 egg

150g ricotta

zest and juice of ½ a lemon

190g plain flour

½ tsp baking powder

½ tsp bicarbonate of soda

PREP

Preheat the oven to 250°C (fan 230°C) and line a large baking sheet with grease-proof paper. If you have one, an ice-cream scoop is handy for portioning out the biscuits.

—

START THE CLOCK

Cream together the butter and sugar until pale and fluffy. Add the rest of the wet ingredients, holding back a little of the lemon zest for decoration.

Then sieve in the flour, baking powder and bicarbonate of soda and stir well to combine.

Using an ice-cream scoop or a pair of dessert spoons, take portions of the mixture – around the size of a ping-pong ball – and space them out on the baking sheet, neatening them up if you have time.

Bake on the top shelf of the oven for 4 minutes, then switch the heat off and leave them for around half an hour to cool inside the oven, with the door slightly ajar.

Serve warm, with the remaining lemon zest sprinkled on top. If you don't eat them straight away, they'll keep for 3 to 4 days in an airtight tin.

CHAPTER 3:

no-bake bakes

Baking doesn't always require an oven – or a microwave.
From a fruity fool to a showstopping pie, my no-bake bakes
are creative, colourful and full of fun

Butterscotch banoffee pie ⬦ Caramel biscuit bites
⬦ Zesty lemon cookies ⬦ Cherry fool ⬦ Mint choc mallow mousse
⬦ Fudgey coffee brownies ⬦ Peanut biscuit squares
⬦ Raspberry ruffle bars ⬦ Chewy flapjacks ⬦ Berry blondies

BUTTERSCOTCH BANOFFEE PIE

Angel Delight, that school dinner staple of the 1960s and 70s, is a retro classic – and much like Marmite, you either love it or hate it. Made by whisking cold milk into sweetened powder to magic up an instant dessert, it's having something of a revival of late . . . and this super-speedy recipe transforms it into a spectacular pudding (that nobody will guess came partly from a packet).

 SERVES 8

120g dark chocolate

10 digestive biscuits (approx. 150g)

150ml dulce de leche or caramel sauce

1 large or 2 small bananas, peeled and sliced

300ml semi-skimmed milk

1 pack of instant butterscotch whipped pudding (59g)

 PREP

Grease a large round pie or flan dish (mine is 25cm diameter) with a little butter. You'll also need a Pyrex bowl, either a food processor or a rolling pin and ziplock bag for crushing the biscuits, a whisk, and a potato peeler or grater for making chocolate curls.

 START THE CLOCK

Put 110g of the chocolate in the Pyrex bowl and melt it in the microwave on high in bursts of 20 seconds at a time (or you can melt it by suspending the bowl over a pan of boiling water if you prefer).

While it melts, crush the digestives to crumbs by blitzing them in a food processor – or you can put them in a ziplock bag and bash them with a rolling pin.

Mix the melted chocolate and biscuit crumbs together and transfer the mixture to the greased dish, using the back of a spoon to press it down firmly into the base and up against the sides.

Spread the caramel over the base, and arrange the slices of banana on top.

Whisk the milk into the butterscotch powder for a minute or so until it thickens, and then spread this over the top of the banoffee mixture.

Take the remaining 10g of chocolate and, using your potato peeler or grater, sprinkle chocolate curls over the top of the pudding.

Put it in the fridge to set for at least half an hour before serving – and if you're not eating it straight away, keep it chilled and it will last 2 or 3 days.

CARAMEL BISCUIT BITES

Biscoff are those little golden-coloured biscuits that come in packs of two on the side of your coffee at the hairdresser's or on a plane. I was over the moon when I discovered you could buy entire packets of them at the supermarket. They give these bites a really lovely burnt caramel flavour, enhanced by plenty of salted caramel sauce.

MAKES 16

175g Biscoff biscuits (approx. 22)

100g white chocolate, broken into pieces

50g salted butter

100g shop-bought salted caramel sauce

40g mini marshmallows (or large ones, quartered)

 PREP

Lay two sheets of cling film, slightly overlapping one another on the longest side, on a chopping board or flat surface. You'll need this for wrapping up your bites. You'll also need a food processor, or a ziplock bag and a rolling pin, for crushing the biscuits and a Pyrex bowl for melting the chocolate.

 START THE CLOCK

Put the biscuits in the food processor and blitz until they turn to crumbs. Alternatively, put them in a ziplock bag and bash them with a rolling pin until they break up – or use the end of a rolling pin to crush them to pieces in a large bowl.

Meanwhile, put the chocolate and butter in the Pyrex bowl and melt them in 20-second bursts on high in the microwave (or over a pan of boiling water if you prefer). Place a sheet of kitchen paper over the top of the bowl to stop the butter from spurting everywhere. It shouldn't take more than 80 seconds to melt.

Tip the biscuit crumbs into a large bowl and add the melted butter mixture, as well as the salted caramel. Mix well. Finally, add the marshmallows.

The mixture should come together into a sticky ball. Transfer this on to the sheets of cling film and, wrapping one over the top of the mix, roll it into a long cylinder. The thickness is up to you – I usually keep mine at a diameter of 5–6cm.

Wrap the cylinder up in the cling film and flatten the ends. Keep rolling until it's neat and you've got it to the desired thickness.

Transfer the cylinder on the board to the fridge and leave it to chill for at least 3 hours. Once hard, use a sharp knife to slice it into discs.

These will keep in the fridge or an airtight container for up to a week.

ZESTY LEMON COOKIES

These raw cookies are packed full of zesty lemon and creamy cashews, which give them a lovely nutty, crumbly texture. You can roll them into balls if you prefer, but I like squashing them into bite-sized biscuits. My secret ingredient is a few squares of white chocolate, which add just the right amount of sweetness to offset that tangy taste.

 MAKES 12

150g cashew nuts

50g oat flour (or ordinary rolled oats, blitzed in a food processor until fine)

100g soft pitted dates

50g desiccated coconut

½ tsp vanilla extract

zest and juice of 1 lemon

30g white chocolate, chopped into tiny chunks

 PREP

Boil the kettle. A food processor or blender will also come in handy for this recipe; otherwise there's a lot of chopping involved. Prepare a plate or board lined with greaseproof paper for chilling your cookies.

—

 START THE CLOCK

Put the cashews in a bowl and cover them completely with boiling water. This will soften them and ensure they're really creamy when you blitz everything up.

Put the oat flour, dates, coconut, vanilla extract and lemon zest and juice in the food processor and whiz for a couple of minutes until everything starts coming together.

Drain the cashews and add them to the food processor. Blitz again – the mixture should start to get nice and creamy.

Finally, add the chopped chocolate. The heat from the cashews will help it melt and stick the rest of the ingredients together. Tip the mixture out into a bowl.

Using your hands – slightly damp palms help here – roll the cookie dough into twelve small balls. Lay these on your plate or board and squash them down into round cookie shapes.

Put them in the fridge or a cool place to chill for an hour or so. They're best kept in the fridge – and should last for up to a week.

CHERRY FOOL

Traditionally, a fruit fool is made by blending stewed fruit with creamy custard, though many modern recipes use whipped cream instead. Mine is a lighter version, made with Greek yoghurt, and I use tart tinned cherries – rippled through the foamy fool – for the ultimate bittersweet dessert.

 MAKES 4

200g tinned drained black cherries (it's worth sieving them just to make sure you've got rid of all the liquid)

1 tbsp honey

50g icing sugar

200g low-fat Greek yoghurt

1 tsp vanilla extract

200ml double or whipping cream

 PREP

Clean and dry your serving dishes – I use ramekins (approx. 200ml capacity), but small bowls or glasses work well too. You'll also need a whisk.

 START THE CLOCK

Put the drained cherries in a large bowl with the honey, holding back four for decoration. Using a fork or potato masher, squash them so they release their lovely purple juices. Leave them there to macerate for approximately 4 minutes.

Meanwhile, sieve the icing sugar over the yoghurt. Add the vanilla extract and whisk to combine.

In a separate bowl, whisk the cream until it forms soft peaks. Fold this into the yoghurt mixture until it's smooth and thick.

When the cherries are soft and the sugar has dissolved, spoon them into the rest of the fool, stirring gently but not mixing fully, so you end up with rich red and purple swirls.

Divide the fool between the serving dishes and top each one with a whole cherry.

Serve chilled. They're best eaten on the day they're made, but will keep for 2 to 3 days in the fridge.

 TIP

For an exotic twist, try making this using coconut yoghurt instead of plain Greek yoghurt. It works well with other tinned fruit, too, like gooseberries or stewed rhubarb.

MINT CHOC MALLOW MOUSSE

Mint chocolate is, I think, one of the most underrated flavours. My pillowy, velvety mousse is made from melted marshmallows and whipped cream – so not only is it free from raw egg whites but it sets in record time. I like to make it in a big bowl and plonk it in the middle of the table for everyone to dig in, but you can decant it into daintier dishes if you prefer.

 SERVES 4

250g dark chocolate, broken into pieces

150g white marshmallows (mini ones or big ones, quartered)

60g unsalted butter

60ml boiling water

300ml double or whipping cream

2 tsp peppermint extract

More whipped cream, fresh mint and broken-up After Eight chocolates to serve

 PREP

Place a medium saucepan over a medium heat on the hob. Make sure you have a large, pretty serving bowl to hand. An electric whisk will also come in handy for beating the cream.

 START THE CLOCK

Put the chocolate, marshmallows, butter and boiling water in the pan and heat, stirring frequently, until everything's smooth and melted together.

Meanwhile, in a large bowl, whisk the cream with the peppermint extract. You want it nice and thick but not solid, so keep going until it forms soft peaks.

Take the mallow mixture off the heat and pour it into the cream. Stir well until everything's combined. You'll need to work quickly, as it will start to thicken up already.

Transfer the mousse to your serving dish (or dishes) and place it in the fridge or a cold place for at least 2 hours until set.

Once it's ready, top with whipped cream, sprigs of fresh mint and shards of After Eight – the perfect dinner party treat. It should keep, covered, for 4 to 5 days in the fridge.

FUDGEY COFFEE BROWNIES

Gooey and chocolatey, but at the same time healthy and packed full of nuts, these no-bake brownies are great if you fancy something sweet yet not overly indulgent. They win you over in stages: the first bite is a zingy hit of coffee, then nuts and then you're left with the flavour of sweet, smooth dates.

 MAKES 25

75g walnuts

100g hazelnuts

50g cocoa powder

1 tsp of coffee powder
(you can grind granules
into powder using a pestle
and mortar)

a pinch of sea salt

225g soft pitted dates

 PREP

Line a small square baking tin (approx. 20cm x 20cm) with greaseproof paper. This recipe will be much easier if you have a food processor – otherwise you've got *a lot* of chopping to do.

 START THE CLOCK

Put 25g of the walnuts and all the hazelnuts into the food processor and blitz until they're finely ground.

Add the cocoa powder, coffee and salt and pulse again. Then transfer to a bowl.

Put the dates into the food processor and blitz into a purée. Add this to the bowl containing the ground nuts and stir thoroughly to combine.

Take the remainder of the walnuts and chop them into chunks (this gives a bit of texture to the brownies) before combining with the rest of the mixture.

Tip the brownie batter out into the prepared tin and press down into the corners so it's tightly packed. Chill in the fridge (for an hour) or freezer (for half an hour) before cutting into pieces.

The brownies are best kept chilled – and should last for up to a week.

PEANUT BISCUIT SQUARES

I came up with these nutty, buttery, biscuity squares while experimenting with flavours for a cheesecake base. Topped with dark chocolate and sea salt, they're not overwhelmingly sweet . . . which is a good thing, as I could eat the whole batch in one sitting.

**MAKES
36 SMALL
SQUARES**

120g salted butter

250g crunchy peanut butter

220g digestive biscuits
(around 13–14)

180g soft dark brown sugar

200g dark chocolate

a sprinkle of sea salt

 PREP

Line a small rectangular baking tray (approx. 20cm x 25cm) with foil. Place a small saucepan on the hob and turn the heat up high. You'll also need a food processor, a Pyrex bowl and a palette knife.

 **START
THE CLOCK**

Put the butter and peanut butter in the saucepan, stir roughly to combine and leave them for a few minutes to melt.

Meanwhile, put the biscuits in the food processor and blitz until they turn to crumbs. (If you don't have a food processor, you can seal them in a ziplock bag and bash them with a rolling pin – but it'll take longer.) Add the sugar and whiz for another minute, before tipping the mixture into a bowl.

Break the chocolate into pieces and melt it in the Pyrex bowl – either in 20-second bursts in the microwave, stirring between each so it doesn't burn, or suspended over a pan of boiling water. Set it aside to cool slightly.

Pour the melted butters over the biscuit crumbs and mix until fully combined. Tip this into the lined tray and press the mixture down into the edges and corners, using the back of a spoon.

Pour the melted chocolate over the top and use the palette knife, dipped in boiling water, to smooth the surface. Finish with a liberal sprinkling of sea salt.

Place it in the fridge for 1 to 2 hours to set (or, if you're really in a hurry, half an hour in the freezer will do the same job).

Using a sharp knife, slice it into 36 pieces. They'll keep for 3 to 4 days in a tin.

RASPBERRY RUFFLE BARS

Now here's a blast from the past! That vibrant pink coconutty filling, enrobed in thick dark chocolate . . . it can only be a retro raspberry ruffle. My version is slightly more refined: a dainty, no-bake bar topped with chocolate and made with freeze-dried raspberry powder.

MAKES 10

150g desiccated coconut

150g coconut cream – note, this is *not* coconut milk, it's much thicker

2 tbsp coconut oil

2 tbsp runny honey

1 tbsp maple syrup

7g freeze-dried raspberries

150g dark chocolate, broken into pieces

PREP

Grease the sides and base of a small square dish (approx. 20cm x 20cm) with a little flavourless oil. You can line it with tin foil or greaseproof paper if you wish – it may make the bars easier to get out. You'll also need a pestle and mortar, a small Pyrex bowl and a palette knife to hand.

—

START THE CLOCK

Mix the coconut, coconut cream, coconut oil, honey and maple syrup together in a bowl until thoroughly combined.

Put the raspberries in the mortar. Take out 1 heaped teaspoon for decoration at the end and grind the rest until you have a fine, vibrantly pink powder. Add this to the coconut mixture and stir through until the colour is even throughout.

Tip the ruffle base into the prepared dish and press it down firmly.

Melt the chocolate in the Pyrex bowl in the microwave, on high in 20-second bursts, stirring between each (or over a pan of boiling water if you prefer) until it's smooth.

Tip the melted chocolate over the coconut mixture and use the palette knife to smooth the top. Sprinkle the remaining raspberry pieces over the top, in five straight lines (this means they'll be arranged neatly down the ruffle bars when you slice them).

Freeze for half an hour or put in the fridge for a couple of hours to set. They'll keep in the fridge or an airtight tin for 4 to 5 days.

—

TIP

If you can't find freeze-dried raspberries, you can use fresh fruit – but to avoid a very wet mixture, drain off most of the liquid in a sieve before adding them to the coconut mixture.

CHEWY FLAPJACKS

Stick-in-your-teeth chewy, but sweetened with healthy coconut oil and honey rather than butter and syrup, these fruity flapjacks are a tasty work/school/any-time-of-the-day-or-night snack. They're studded with nuts and fruit, so they're more interesting than plain old oats – and worryingly addictive.

MAKES ABOUT 20

50g coconut oil (I like the flavour this gives, but you can use unsalted butter if you prefer)

120ml runny honey

½ tsp vanilla extract

a pinch of mixed spice

150g finely milled porridge oats

140g mixed nuts (I use cashews, pecans and almonds), roughly chopped

140g cranberries (or other dried fruit if you prefer)

PREP

Place a medium saucepan over a high heat on the hob. Line a large rectangular dish (mine is 20cm x 30cm, and around 5cm deep) with tin foil, pressing it tightly into the corners. A palette knife will also come in handy.

START THE CLOCK

Put the coconut oil or butter, honey, vanilla extract and mixed spice in the pan. Stir together and heat until it melts and starts to foam.

Turn the heat down and add the rest of the ingredients to the pan, stirring gently so they're well mixed. Allow them to cook – which will soften everything and help it stick together – for 3 to 4 minutes.

Tip the flapjack mix into the prepared dish and spread it evenly over the base.

Using the palette knife or a clean palm – but be careful, as it can still be quite hot! – press the mixture very firmly down into the dish. This step is crucial – you want everything to be very tightly compacted or your flapjacks will fall apart, even when they're cool.

Put the dish in the fridge or a cold place to harden for around 2 hours.

When they're set, slice the flapjacks into 20 bars using a sharp knife. Store for up to a week in an airtight container.

BERRY BLONDIES

These nutty, no-bake blondies are (dare I say it) verging on healthy, so packed full are they of nuts, dates and nutritious almond butter. But don't worry, they still taste delicious – and for good measure I've topped them with berries and plenty of artfully spattered white chocolate.

MAKES 24

275g pecan nuts

120g almond butter

2 tbsp maple syrup

¼ tsp sea salt

300g soft pitted dates

100g white chocolate, broken into pieces

300g fresh berries (any variety, or a mixture, will do)

PREP

Line a large rectangular baking dish (approx. 20cm x 30cm) with tin foil, pressing it into the corners and up the sides so your blondies will have neat edges. You'll also need a food processor, a palette knife or large spoon, and a Pyrex bowl for melting the chocolate.

START THE CLOCK

Put the pecans into the food processor and blitz them until they turn to crumbs. If you don't have a processor, you can finely chop them with a sharp knife – just keep going until the bits are really tiny.

While the pecans are being blitzed, mix the almond butter, maple syrup and salt together in a bowl. Tip in the ground nuts and stir to combine.

Whiz the dates in the food processor and keep pulsing until they start coming together into a big sticky ball. Scrape the mixture into the bowl with the other ingredients and mix well.

Tip the blondie batter into the prepared dish, pressing it down with the palette knife or the back of the spoon until you have a nice smooth top.

Melt the chocolate in the Pyrex bowl – either by blasting it in 20-second bursts in the microwave or by suspending it over a pan of boiling water. Scatter the berries over the top of the blondies and drizzle over the melted chocolate, channelling your inner Jackson Pollock.

Put the dish in the fridge for a few hours, or set it in a cool place, to let everything firm up before slicing and serving. The blondies will keep for 3 to 4 days in the fridge.

CHAPTER 4:

cheats' treats

Baking up a storm in minutes is all about clever cheats,
from doughnuts made with puff pastry to crème brûlées
topped with shop-bought toffees

Cinnamon cronuts ⋄ Oreo cheesecake parfaits
⋄ Eton mess fridge cake ⋄ Panettone perdu
⋄ Cheats' crème brûlées ⋄ Top-speed tiramisu ⋄ Skillet flambé
⋄ Golden Nutella ravioli ⋄ Gooey coffee pots ⋄ Feta filo rolls

CINNAMON CRONUTS

All the satisfying stodge of a doughnut but with the flaky layers of a croissant? It's hard to think of a more devilish – or mouth-watering – combination than the 'cronut', invented by New York-based pastry chef Dominique Ansel in 2013. Here's my take on this baking mash-up: pillowy puffs of pastry rolled in crisp cinnamon sugar, best eaten piping hot.

**MAKES
9–12**

800ml sunflower or vegetable oil (for frying)

1 x 320g shop-bought ready-rolled puff pastry sheet

100g caster sugar

3 tsp ground cinnamon

 PREP

Pour the oil into a medium pan (you want it to come around two-thirds up the sides of the pan) and put it on the hob over a high heat. It should take 8–10 minutes to get to the right temperature (approx. 180°C). Check it's hot enough by dropping a tiny ball of pastry or a crumb of bread into the oil: if it sizzles and floats to the top, the oil's ready.

You'll also need a 6cm round cutter to cut the pastry – or two of different sizes if you'd prefer to make ring cronuts – and a slotted spoon to take the cronuts out of the hot oil.

 **START
THE CLOCK**

Roll out the sheet of puff pastry and fold it in half across the length to make a smaller rectangle. Press the two layers down with the heel of your hand so they stick and don't come apart.

Using the cutter, cut circles out of the doubled pastry sheet. There should be enough for around nine on the first go, and if you're re-rolling the pastry, do it gently so it doesn't lose its puff. To make ring cronuts, cut a hole inside the larger circle with a smaller cutter (around 3cm diameter).

Drop the discs, six at a time, into the hot oil. Be careful – it's extremely hot, so either use a pan guard to stop it spattering or keep your face and hands at a safe distance.

Let them bubble away for around a minute on one side before flipping them over. While they cook, mix the sugar and cinnamon together in a large bowl.

Using a slotted spoon, transfer the cronuts directly from the pan to the bowl and roll them in the sugar. Drop the remaining pastry discs into the oil and repeat.

Eat hot, drizzled with icing or melted chocolate, or with a salted caramel dip on the side. They'll keep for 4 to 5 days in an airtight tin.

 TIP —

Don't dispose of the hot oil immediately. Place the pan somewhere safe, where there's no risk of the handle being knocked or tipped, and let it cool completely. You can decant it back into the bottle to use again, or save it in an old bottle to take to your local recycling centre.

OREO CHEESECAKE PARFAITS

Oreo cookies plus the speediest cheesecake mix you've ever met equals . . . pure deliciousness! These little parfaits combine fluffy clouds of sweet, creamy cheesecake whip with crunchy layers of crumbled Oreo cookie. Perfect for a swanky party (or an indulgent TV dinner for one).

 SERVES 4

2 x 250g tubs of low-fat cream cheese

100g icing sugar

½ tsp vanilla extract

300ml double or whipping cream

1 packet Oreo cookies (13–14 biscuits)

 PREP

Clean and dry four glasses or dishes to serve your parfaits in. I use tumblers – transparent ones are best so you can appreciate the layers – of approx. 300ml capacity. Put them in the fridge to chill. You'll also need a whisk – manual or electric, though a hand whisk is best as it ensures you won't over-work the cream.

 START THE CLOCK

In a large bowl, beat the cream cheese, icing sugar and vanilla extract until smooth.

Pour the cream into a separate bowl and whisk it until it forms soft peaks. Gradually fold the whipped cream into the cream cheese mixture, trying to keep as much air in it as possible so it's light and bubbly.

Crumble the cookies into a bowl. You can either use your hands or bash them with a rolling pin – you want to end up with a mixture of crumbs and larger chunks.

Now it's time to assemble the parfaits. Take the glasses out of the fridge and fill them with alternating layers of ingredients, starting with the cheesecake mix and finishing with a liberal sprinkling of cookie crumbs.

Serve immediately – or, if you want to make them ahead of time, keep the two elements separate, with the cheesecake mix well covered in the fridge, and assemble just before serving. It will keep, well chilled, for a couple of days.

ETON MESS FRIDGE CAKE

A fridge cake can only be loosely called a 'cake' – it mostly comprises chocolate, butter and whipped cream, studded with chunks of biscuit and other odds and ends, and is 'baked' by placing it in the fridge to set. Mine is a play on the classic British dessert Eton mess, which dates back to 1893.

 MAKES 25 SQUARES

150g white chocolate, broken into pieces

30g unsalted butter

130ml double cream

30g meringue, crushed (ready-made nests will do, or you can make your own if you've got time on your hands)

75g dried red fruit (traditionally, strawberries or raspberries are used, but I like cranberries, too)

85g shortbread fingers, crushed (or you can use Jammie Dodgers)

 PREP

Line a small square baking tray (20cm x 20cm, 5cm deep) with tin foil, pressing it into the corners so your fridge cake will have neat edges. You'll also need a Pyrex bowl, a whisk and a palette knife.

—

 START THE CLOCK

Put the chocolate and butter into the Pyrex bowl and melt – either in the microwave on high in 20-second bursts or suspended over a pan of boiling water.

Whisk the cream to soft peaks while the chocolate and butter cool slightly, then fold into the melted mixture, stirring until all the lumps have disappeared.

Stir in all but a handful of the meringue, dried fruit and crushed shortbread fingers and transfer the fridge cake mix to the prepared tin, using the palette knife to spread and flatten it out.

Top with the remaining bits, pressing these down so they stick.

Put the cake in the fridge for 3 to 4 hours to set, before slicing it into 25 small squares or triangles.

It's incredibly sweet, so works well served with coffee after a big meal, and will keep in the fridge for up to a week.

PANETTONE PERDU

Pain perdu – the posh name for French toast – is a classic dish: crisp and buttery on the outside, soft and creamy on the inside. My recipe takes bog-standard eggy bread to a whole new level, with slices of panettone – the fruity Italian loaf usually eaten at Christmas – soaked in sweet custard.

 SERVES 2

2 eggs

200ml whole milk or cream

20g caster sugar

zest of 1 orange

1 tsp ground nutmeg

1 tsp vanilla extract

2 thick-cut slices of panettone

For the fruity syrup:

2 oranges: use the juice from one half and slice the other into segments

60g caster sugar

80g cranberries

 PREP

Put a knob of butter in a large, non-stick frying pan and place it on the hob over a medium-high heat. Place a small saucepan over a medium heat and get it nice and warm. You'll also need a whisk.

START THE CLOCK

In a wide, deep bowl, whisk the eggs, milk, sugar, orange zest, nutmeg and vanilla extract together.

Lay the slices of panettone flat in the bowl and leave them for a few seconds on each side to soak up plenty of custard.

Transfer the panettone to the frying pan. Leave the slices to sizzle for 2 minutes, before flipping to the other side. They should be crisp and golden on the side that's cooked.

Meanwhile, put the orange juice and caster sugar in the small saucepan and heat together until the sugar dissolves and starts bubbling. After a couple of minutes, add the orange segments and cranberries and leave them to stew for a minute or two.

When the panettone is ready, arrange each slice on a plate and top with the hot zesty syrup.

This is best eaten straight after cooking, but you can keep it in the fridge for 1 or 2 days and reheat in the microwave or a hot pan before serving.

CHEATS' CRÈME BRÛLÉES

Crème brûlée, also known as 'burnt cream', popped up on the menu at Trinity College, Cambridge, in 1879. Known for its buttery smooth centre and that satisfying 'crack' from the caramelized sugar on top, it's one of the nation's favourite desserts. My cheats' version swaps the traditional egg custard for a lighter alternative, and uses a clever workaround to create that crunchy topping.

 MAKES 4

150g blackberries

30g caster sugar

zest of ½ a lemon

200g crème fraîche

200g Greek yoghurt

120g Werther's Original sweets (or other boiled toffees), chopped into tiny pieces

 PREP

Grease four ramekins or small serving dishes (approx. 200ml capacity). Preheat the grill to high and put a small saucepan on the hob over a medium heat.

 START THE CLOCK

Put the blackberries, sugar and lemon zest in the pan and heat for a few minutes, until the berries start softening and releasing their juices.

Meanwhile, mix the crème fraîche and yoghurt in a bowl. Then spoon the berry mixture into the prepared ramekins, equally dividing the fruit and juice. Cover with the yoghurt mixture and smooth it down.

Sprinkle the chopped sweets on top, making sure the white layer is completely covered. It helps if the sweets are in tiny pieces, almost like a fine powder (you can use a food processor to blitz them if chopping only gets you so far).

Transfer the ramekins to the top shelf of the grill and cook for 3 minutes, until the sweets on top are melted and bubbling. If you've got one and know how to use it safely, a hand-held blowtorch will also work to caramelize the tops.

Give the caramel 10 to 15 minutes to set hard before serving.

These can be eaten hot or cold and will keep for 2 to 3 days in the fridge – though you may wish to give the tops another blast under a hot grill.

 TIP

Any other variety of soft, sharp fruit works just as well in this recipe – try raspberries or blueberries, and grated orange or lime rind. And if you're feeling really lazy, substitute the crème fraîche and yoghurt for shop-bought custard.

TOP-SPEED TIRAMISU

I have a confession to make: I don't actually like tiramisu. Too much dairy, too much effort – and too many bad, bland experiences. But my husband tells me I'm mad – and I realize I'm in the minority – so I've come up with a lightning-quick version that is lighter, tastier and packed full of punchy espresso. The result? A creamy, dreamy dessert that can convince even haters like me.

 SERVES 6

300ml double or whipping cream

75g caster sugar

1 tsp vanilla extract

250g mascarpone cheese

150ml cheats' espresso (2 heaped tbsp instant coffee dissolved in 150ml hot water)

1 x 175g packet of sponge fingers (or plain vanilla cake/loaf/cup-cakes, cut into 1cm-thick slices)

20g cocoa powder

optional: add a dash of brandy, Bailey's or amaretto to the coffee to give it a kick

 PREP

You'll need a 20cm-square, 5cm-deep serving dish. I find this works well if you stick the dish in the fridge to chill beforehand – this helps to cool the contents, keeping the layers neat.

You'll also need an electric whisk (if you don't have one, a hand whisk will do) and a piping bag or large sandwich bag.

 START THE CLOCK

In a large bowl, whisk the cream, sugar and vanilla extract to soft peaks. Use a spoon to break up the mascarpone cheese and then whisk this into the mixture.

Put the espresso mixture in a separate bowl and dunk the fingers, very quickly, in the hot coffee so that you don't end up with soggy biscuits.

Lay half of the soaked sponge fingers over the base of the serving dish and top with a third of the cream mixture, followed by a dusting of half the cocoa powder.

Repeat the sponge finger layer. Transfer the remaining two-thirds of the cream mixture to the piping bag (or put it in the sandwich bag, squeeze it down and snip off one corner of the bag to make a 2cm hole) and pipe blobs of it neatly over the top of the fingers. Top with a dusting of cocoa.

Place the tiramisu in the fridge until you're ready to serve. It should keep, chilled and covered, for 4 to 5 days but is best eaten on the day it's made.

SKILLET FLAMBÉ

This dreamy, indulgent dessert is made in one pan – a deep cast-iron skillet (hence the name). If you don't have one, you can use a frying pan, but I love how retro this looks and how the bananas fit snugly in the blanket of caramel sauce. Alcohol is optional, but a real flambé needs a fiery flame!

 SERVES 2

25g unsalted butter

50g soft light brown or caster sugar

30g chopped pecan nuts

½ tsp vanilla extract

½ tsp ground cinnamon

2 small bananas (approx. 100g each), peeled and cut in half lengthways

optional: 1 tsp brandy, dark rum or bourbon – any spirit will do as long as it's 40% alcohol or higher

 PREP

You'll need a skillet (mine is 20cm across, 5cm deep and has cast-iron handles). But if you don't have one, a small frying pan will do (not too big or the sauce will cook too quickly). Preheat it on a medium-high heat.

You'll also need a box of long matches or a long-handled lighter, so you can keep your distance from that flame.

 START THE CLOCK

Put the butter and sugar in the pan. Stir constantly until they're melted and the sugar has started to caramelize; it shouldn't take longer than a minute or two.

Add the chopped nuts, vanilla extract and cinnamon, mix well and finally lay the bananas on top. Arrange them so as much banana as possible is immersed in the sauce – I put them cut-side down to start, sitting snugly inside one another.

After 2 minutes, gently flip the bananas and cook them for another minute. If you're making the non-alcoholic version, stop here: your flambé is ready to serve.

But if you're adding the alcohol, pour it over the top now and – making sure there's plenty of room and you're not cooking in an enclosed space – carefully hold the long match or lighter to the alcohol to ignite it.

There should be a brief (but pretty spectacular) flame, which will burn off in seconds – if you want, you can do this step at the table so everyone gets to see.

Serve immediately, with scoops of ice cream or yoghurt to cool down the boozy hot sauce.

GOLDEN NUTELLA RAVIOLI

Crunchy, golden and delicious, deep-fried ravioli started life as a savoury dish, made popular in the Italian neighbourhoods of St Louis, Missouri. I've turned it into a sweet showstopper, filled with hot melty chocolate spread and covered in crunchy hazelnuts.

 MAKES 16

300ml sunflower or vegetable oil (for frying)

4 fresh lasagne sheets

8 tsp Nutella or other chocolate spread

2 eggs, beaten

50g finely chopped hazelnuts

1 tbsp icing sugar, for dusting

 PREP

Pour the oil into a large, shallow frying pan; it should be 1–2 cm deep. It's best in a pan with a lid or a spatter guard to protect you against splashes. Put the pan over a medium-high heat and heat the oil to around 180°C – you'll know it's ready when a crumb of pastry or bread dropped in sizzles and turns brown in seconds.

It's also a good idea to prepare a plate with a few sheets of kitchen paper, and to find a pastry brush and a slotted spoon for removing your ravioli from the oil.

Finally, you'll need a pasta cutter (these look like mini pizza cutters), preferably with a fluted edge. If you don't have one, a sharp knife will do.

 START THE CLOCK

Stack the lasagne sheets on top of one another and slice them into eight squares: make one cut lengthways and three across. Each raviolo is formed from two squares of pasta, one on top of the other, so there should be enough to make sixteen.

Lay them out in pairs so they're easy to assemble. Put half a teaspoon of Nutella in the centre of one square of pasta. Take the other square and brush one side with beaten egg, then lay it, egg side down, over the Nutella square. Squeeze the edges together and use the prongs of a fork to seal it.

Finally, dip the sealed raviolo in more beaten egg, and then lay each side in the chopped hazelnuts so they stick. Then carefully transfer them to the hot oil.

Fry the ravioli for 1 minute on each side, using the slotted spoon to flip them over once they turn golden brown. Don't worry if they open a little. When they're all done, transfer them to the plate covered in kitchen paper to soak up any excess oil.

Dust them with icing sugar and serve hot, oozing gooey Nutella. They won't really keep, so eat them all in one go or share them around.

GOOEY COFFEE POTS

Do you ever fancy something sweet but feel like you need a great big whack of coffee at the same time? These little coffee pots – hot and gooey in the middle, light and fluffy on the outside – are just that: packed full of energy-boosting caffeine but sophisticated enough to serve as a dessert.

 MAKES 4

2 tsp instant coffee

160ml chocolate milk

50g unsalted butter, softened

50g caster sugar

25g self-raising flour

50g ground almonds

25g cocoa powder

a pinch of salt

1 egg

 PREP

Grease four ramekins or espresso cups (approx. 180ml capacity) with a little butter. You'll also need a hand whisk.

—

START THE CLOCK

Mix the instant coffee into the chocolate milk and whisk until dissolved. It may need a quick blast (10 to 20 seconds) in the microwave to speed things along.

In a separate bowl, mix together the rest of the ingredients. Start by creaming together the butter and sugar, then add the dry ingredients and beat in the egg.

Add the coffee mixture, a little at a time, stirring until it's completely combined.

Divide the batter between your prepared pots – it should go around halfway up each one.

Microwave these all together on high for 3.5 to 4 minutes. The longer they cook, the less gooey they'll be, so keep an eye on them and stop baking when you reckon they're just done.

Serve hot, in their ramekins, topped with a scoop of ice cream.

They'll keep in the fridge for a couple of days; just reheat them (1 minute in the microwave) before serving. Or you can enjoy them cold.

—

 TIP

For the ultimate coffee-lovers' treat, why not top these with an affogato? Spoon on a scoop of vanilla ice cream and then, just before serving, pour on a single (or double) shot of hot espresso. It'll melt the ice cream and create a delicious creamy coffee sauce for your pud.

FETA FILO ROLLS

Spinach and feta pie is a classic Greek dish, combining the creaminess of the cheese with crisp, golden pastry. My filo rolls use the same paper-thin pastry, which comes in handy packs from the supermarket, but rolled around a feta filling, zinged up with lemon zest and plenty of seasoning.

MAKES 12

250ml sunflower or vegetable oil (for frying)

60g baby spinach leaves, steamed and chopped

75g feta cheese

zest of ½ a lemon

½ tsp each of salt and pepper

2 large sheets of shop-bought filo pastry

1 egg

 PREP

You'll need a large shallow frying pan with a lid or spatter guard. Pour in the oil and put it on the hob over a high heat for around 8 to 10 minutes. Check it's ready by dropping a crumb of filo into the hot oil: if it sizzles and turns golden in less than a minute, you're good to go.

Prepare your frying station by lining a side plate or board with plenty of kitchen paper to soak up the excess oil, and have a slotted spoon to hand.

 START THE CLOCK

Mash the spinach into the feta, along with the lemon zest and seasoning. Set aside.

Lay one sheet of filo pastry out flat. Whisk the egg with a fork and brush it over the top of the pastry before laying the second sheet on top and sticking it down.

Using a sharp knife, cut the layered pastry into twelve – three cuts across the sheet and two lengthways – to make evenly sized rectangles.

Put a dollop of feta mixture at the short end of each pastry rectangle and lightly brush the rest of the dough with egg. Starting at the end where the filling is, roll tightly into a cylinder, pinching either end, so it doesn't squeeze out.

Using a slotted spoon, transfer the filo rolls to the hot oil and put the lid or spatter guard on. Give them a minute on one side before carefully flipping to the other, and then use the spoon to move them to the plate covered in kitchen paper.

Serve hot or cold, as party nibbles or a starter, either on their own or with a bowl of sweet chilli sauce or spicy tomato salsa for dipping. They'll keep for around 5 days in the fridge, but may need crisping up in the oven if you don't eat them straight away.

CHAPTER 5:

breakfast bites

Some days, cornflakes just won't cut it. From cornbread and cheesy muffins to spiced omelettes and microwave shakshuka, start your day with a bang!

American cornbread ◇ Microwave shakshuka
◇ Cinnamon raisin wholewheat scone ◇ Rarebit muffins
◇ Savoury French toastie ◇ Fluffy drop scones with maple butter
◇ Bounty baked oats with nut butter ◇ Oaty breakfast cups
◇ Dill pancakes with salmon ◇ Spicy sweet potato latkes ◇ Masala omelette

AMERICAN CORNBREAD

Fluffy, gloriously yellow and sweet and salty at the same time, cornbread is a popular breakfast dish in the southern states of America, where it's baked, fried and even steamed. My version starts life in the microwave – and tastes great served up with crispy bacon and scrambled egg.

 SERVES 4–6

75g plain flour

75g polenta (or cornmeal, both made from finely milled yellow maize)

40g caster sugar

2 tsp baking powder

½ tsp each of salt and pepper

2 tbsp vegetable oil

1 egg

130ml semi-skimmed milk

 PREP

Grease a square, microwave- and ovenproof dish (mine is 20cm x 20cm) with a little oil, and preheat the grill to high.

—

 START THE CLOCK

Mix the dry ingredients in one bowl, and the wet ingredients in another bowl.

Once they're fully combined, mix the two together and stir thoroughly. Transfer the cornbread batter to the prepared dish.

Microwave it on high for 3 minutes, rotating the dish halfway through if it's too big to spin inside the microwave.

Using oven gloves (it will be piping hot), transfer the microwaved bread to the top shelf of the grill and cook for a further 2 minutes. This will give it a nice crisp topping.

Serve immediately, with your favourite breakfast accompaniments. If you're making it ahead of time, the cornbread will keep for 3 to 4 days in an airtight tin.

MICROWAVE SHAKSHUKA

Originally made in the Middle East and across the Mediterranean, shakshuka is one of my go-to breakfast dishes: runny eggs poached in a spicy, aromatic sauce of tomatoes, peppers, cumin and paprika. It can take a good hour to make, but you can make my version in just six minutes – meaning you don't even have to save it for lazy weekend mornings.

SERVES 2–4 (DEPENDING ON HOW HUNGRY YOU ARE!)

1 red pepper, chopped into 1cm cubes

1 tbsp olive oil

1 tsp each of:
    garlic granules (or 2 cloves, finely diced)
    cumin seeds
    smoked paprika
    Tabasco (or other hot pepper sauce)

½ a vegetable stock cube dissolved in 30ml boiling water

1 x 400g tin of chopped tomatoes

4 eggs

To serve:

a handful of crumbled feta cheese

a handful of torn parsley

pitta breads or toasted sourdough

PREP

Clean and dry a 20cm-round microwaveable dish.

—

START THE CLOCK

Put the chopped pepper, oil and spices (including the hot sauce) into the dish and stir to combine.

Mix the stock into the chopped tomatoes and pour this mixture over the top of the pepper pieces. Give everything a good stir and microwave on high for 30 seconds.

Using a teaspoon, make four little wells in the tomato mixture and crack an egg into each. Don't worry if some of the white overflows; but try to keep most of the egg immersed in the sauce, as this helps it to poach evenly.

Microwave the entire dish on high for 5 minutes, watching carefully so the eggs don't overcook. It's ready when the white has just turned opaque and the yolks are still nice and wobbly.

Top with feta and parsley and serve immediately, straight from the dish if you like, with big hunks of bread to soak up all that delicious sauce.

TIP

So as not to waste any of that tomato goodness, I like to make my stock in the tin itself. Just tip out the tomatoes, drop in the stock cube and pour in the boiling water, giving it all a good swirl to dissolve the stock and get the tomato juice off the sides and base of the tin.

CINNAMON RAISIN WHOLEWHEAT SCONE

This isn't just any scone . . . it's a giant scone, baked the old-fashioned way in one big round and then sliced into pieces like a pizza. Made from ground oats and chia seeds rather than flour (meaning it's gluten-free), it's got a wholewheat, nutty texture, studded with cinnamon-spiced raisins.

 SERVES 8

175g rolled oats

4 tbsp chia seeds (you'll find these at any supermarket or health food shop)

2 tsp baking powder

a pinch of salt

240g apple sauce

60ml semi-skimmed milk

75g raisins

1 tbsp ground cinnamon

1 tbsp demerara sugar

 PREP

Grease a 20cm-round microwave-proof dish or tin and line the base with a circle of greaseproof paper (this makes it easier to remove the baked scone). You'll also need a food processor, and a palette knife or large spoon.

 START THE CLOCK

Put the oats, chia seeds, baking powder and salt into the food processor and blitz until they turn to a fine powder. If you don't have a food processor or blender, a pestle and mortar and some elbow grease will do the same job.

Tip the powdered oat mixture into a large bowl and add the rest of the ingredients, except the demerara sugar.

Mix thoroughly to combine before transferring the mixture to the prepared dish. Spread it out and flatten down the top using the palette knife or spoon.

Sprinkle the demerara sugar over the top of the scone (this will give a crisp topping) and, using a sharp knife, score it into roughly eight slices – exactly like a pizza. Microwave on high for 3 minutes.

Once the scone is baked, leave it in the dish for 10 minutes or so before transferring it to a bread board. Go over the scored cuts to slice the scone into eight portions.

You can eat it fresh, sliced in half and slathered with butter and a slab of mature Cheddar. It also tastes delicious with a dollop of clotted cream. Kept in an airtight tin, it should stay fresh for up to a week.

RAREBIT MUFFINS

Is it controversial to have cheese for breakfast? My dad eats toast with marmalade and slices of Cheddar on top . . . so I grew up thinking it's normal. This recipe shows you how to make your own fluffy muffins (gluten-free, no less), topped with gooey Welsh rarebit: a breakfast of kings.

 MAKES 2

80g coconut flour (I use this because it's spongey and absorbent, giving your muffins a lovely texture and flavour, as well as being wheat-free)

60ml semi-skimmed milk

3 eggs

½ tsp baking powder

For the rarebit topping:

110g Cheddar or other hard cheese, grated

2 tbsp semi-skimmed milk

10g salted butter

1 tsp plain flour (you can use coconut flour here if you want to stick to gluten-free)

1 tsp Worcestershire sauce

½ tsp English mustard

plenty of black pepper

 PREP

Grease two large ramekins (mine are 10cm diameter) with butter. Place a medium pan over the hob on a high heat.

 START THE CLOCK

Put the rarebit ingredients (except the pepper) in the pan on the hob and stir thoroughly. Stir frequently as the cheese and butter melt into a gooey mixture.

While this cooks, combine the muffin ingredients in a small bowl and mix with a fork until there are no lumps. Divide the mixture between the two ramekins and use the back of a spoon to press it down.

Microwave on high for 3 minutes – the muffins will puff up. By now the rarebit mixture should have started to bubble.

Invert the ramekins and gently tap the bottom to get the muffins out. Slice them in half – and toast them if you want – before topping with spoonfuls of rarebit and several grinds of black pepper.

These won't keep, so there's no excuse not to eat them straight away!

SAVOURY FRENCH TOASTIE

French toast is, for me, food from the gods. Turning soggy, egg-drenched bread into a golden toasted treat by frying it in a buttery pan is ingenious. But truth be told, I always find it a little bit too sweet. My six-minute recipe combines my two favourite indulgences: French toast and a cheese toastie. Prepare to be transported to breakfast heaven.

 SERVES 2

2 eggs

45ml semi-skimmed milk

20g salted butter, melted

½ tsp each of:
  smoked paprika
  garlic powder
  dried oregano

a pinch of salt and pepper

4 slices brioche or French baguette, cut medium-thick

approx. 100g sliced hard cheese (e.g. mature Cheddar, Gruyère, Emmental)

 PREP

Put a knob of butter in a large frying pan on the hob over a medium-high heat and leave it to melt. You'll also need a whisk and a fish slice.

 START THE CLOCK

First, prepare your French toast batter. Whisk the eggs into the milk and melted butter and add the spices, herbs and seasoning.

Take each slice of bread in turn and dunk both sides in the batter.

Lay two slices on the hot pan – they should sizzle the moment you set them down – and arrange the slices of cheese over the top. Sandwich another slice of dunked bread on top of each toastie.

Using a fish slice or a heavy object (such as a tin or heatproof kitchen implement), apply pressure to the top of the toastie, leaving it to cook for 2 minutes.

Flip and cook on the other side for another 2 minutes. The cheese inside should be just melted, the eggy mixture golden – and the toast perfectly crisp.

Serve hot and tuck in immediately. If you've got time, add some baked beans on the side – and a sprinkle of chopped fresh parsley over the top.

FLUFFY DROP SCONES with MAPLE BUTTER

For a special occasion, weekend brunch or to brighten up a drab Monday, these tasty morsels are just the ticket. They're called 'drop scones' rather than pancakes because they're thicker, fluffier and you can 'drop' them into the pan without worrying that the batter will spread. I prefer them to stodgy American pancakes or thin French crêpes . . . and the whipped butter adds the wow factor.

MAKES 6–8

170g self-raising flour

1 tsp baking powder

1 tsp ground cinnamon

50g soft light brown sugar

1 egg

200ml semi-skimmed milk

a handful of golden raisins
(or chocolate chips, nuts or
blueberries if you prefer)

To serve:

60g salted butter, well softened

2 tsp maple syrup

PREP

Put a small knob of butter in a large frying pan over a medium-high heat. As it melts, swirl it around so it covers the base of the pan.

Prepare a large sheet of tin foil over a plate to keep the drop scones hot between batches. You'll also need a whisk – electric is best, if you have one – a ladle and a fish slice.

START THE CLOCK

Sieve the flour, baking powder and cinnamon into a large bowl and stir in the sugar.

Whisk in the egg followed by the milk, a few glugs at a time, until you have a smooth batter, roughly the consistency of thick double cream.

By now the butter in the pan should be starting to bubble. Use the ladle to transfer large spoonfuls of the batter into the pan, spaced slightly apart. Depending on the size of your pan, there should be enough room for three or four large circles – and this should use up half the batter.

Use the underside of the ladle to neaten them up, and then drop a few raisins (or whatever you're using) on top. Adding them at this stage stops them collecting at the bottom of the bowl or burning on the base of the pan.

While the pancakes cook, put the softened butter into a bowl and whisk it vigorously until it turns white.

It should only take a minute — by which stage the pancakes will be ready to flip, using a fish slice. While that side cooks, add the maple syrup to the whipped butter and whisk for another minute.

Transfer the drop scones to the foil-covered plate and repeat with the remainder of the batter. Serve immediately, topped with spoonfuls of the whipped maple butter.

BOUNTY BAKED OATS
with NUT BUTTER

All the mouth-watering flavours of a Bounty bar . . . for breakfast. What's not to like? This delicious, nutritious recipe is halfway between porridge and an oat muffin, and it's topped with spoonfuls of homemade toasted nut butter. Go on, treat yourself this morning.

 SERVES 1

60g almonds, cashews or peanuts, skins on or off

40g rolled oats

75g natural yoghurt

35ml chocolate milk

1 tbsp caster sugar

1 tbsp cocoa powder

20g desiccated coconut

1 tsp coconut essence

1 egg

a drizzle of flavourless oil, such as sunflower or vegetable oil (if needed)

 PREP

Preheat the oven to 250°C (fan 230°C). You'll need a baking tray for toasting the nuts, a medium-sized microwave-proof bowl, and a food processor for making the nut butter.

 START THE CLOCK

Spread the nuts out on the baking tray and put them in the oven for 5 minutes to toast. As they heat, they release all their lovely oils, essential for blending them into butter.

Meanwhile, make the baked oats. Put all the other ingredients (except the oil) in the bowl and beat vigorously to combine. Put the bowl in the microwave and heat it on high for 2.5–3 minutes.

When the nuts are nice and toasty, tip them into the food processor and blitz them on the fastest setting. They might come together on their own – or, if it all looks a little dry, drizzle in a few drops of oil until it turns to the consistency of butter.

Serve the baked oats hot (be careful – the bowl will be very warm), topped with plenty of homemade nut butter and a dollop of natural yoghurt. Guaranteed to start your day off with a smile.

 TIP

If you've got a whole bag of nuts, don't skimp when making the nut butter. Blitz them all, adding oil as required, and keep the leftovers in a jar in the fridge for up to two weeks. Perfect on toast, porridge or straight from the pot.

OATY BREAKFAST CUPS

These nifty little cups combine everything you might eat at breakfast time: oats, eggs, peanut butter – even some dried fruit – and transform the ingredients into a morning showstopper. Tasty, nutritious and packed with fibre, you can fill them with whatever you desire to start the day.

 MAKES 4

100g rolled oats

2 eggs

2 tbsp nut butter (I use peanut butter but any variety will do)

½ tsp mixed spice

50g dried and pitted dates, finely chopped

To fill the cups:

a few spoonfuls of Greek yoghurt and berries, chopped apple and nuts, or your favourite breakfast cereal and milk

 PREP

Clean and dry four small dishes or ramekins (around 8cm diameter, with a flat bottom) and grease the base and sides with a little butter or oil.

 START THE CLOCK

Mix all the ingredients together in a bowl.

Divide the mixture between the four ramekins and use the back of a spoon to press it down into the base and force it up the sides, creating a cup shape that mirrors the inside of the ramekin.

Microwave them together on high for 3 minutes.

Allow the cups to cool slightly before filling them with your favourite breakfast treats. You can either serve them in the ramekins or, using a blunt knife or spoon to loosen the edges, carefully turn them out.

Filled, you should eat them on the same day (or wrap them up and bring them to work or school). Unfilled, they'll keep for 4 to 5 days in an airtight tin.

DILL PANCAKES with SALMON

Smoked salmon is a breakfast staple in my house, and my dill pancakes are light, fluffy and the perfect match for it, served with zingy crème fraîche with lemon and capers. Better still, this batter doesn't need to rest – so you can use it straight away.

 SERVES 4

150g plain flour

a pinch of salt

2 eggs

250ml milk

a small bunch of dill (approx. 10g), leaves finely chopped, plus a few extra sprigs for serving

1 tbsp capers

zest and juice of 1 lemon

150g crème fraîche

100g smoked salmon

 PREP

Put a knob of butter in a large frying pan over a medium heat and leave it to melt.

Preheat the oven to a low heat (around 80°C or fan 60°C) and prepare a heatproof plate with several sheets of greaseproof paper for keeping the crêpes hot. You'll also need a whisk, a ladle or large spoon and a palette knife or fish slice.

START THE CLOCK

Sieve the flour and salt into a bowl, make a well in the middle and crack in the eggs. Slowly whisk in the milk until the batter is smooth, then stir in the chopped dill.

Using the ladle or large spoon, transfer a quarter of the batter to the frying pan and swirl to make sure it evenly covers the base. Cook for around 30 to 40 seconds on one side before using the palette knife or fish slice to flip it over. Repeat on the other side and then transfer to the plate in the oven.

Repeat with the remainder of the batter, placing sheets of greaseproof paper between the cooked crêpes to stop them going soggy.

While the crêpes cook, mix the capers and lemon zest and juice into the crème fraîche, stirring thoroughly until it's smooth.

Serve hot, with a generous portion of salmon, a dollop of the zingy crème fraîche and a few extra sprigs of dill on the side.

 TIP

If you don't like dill, try substituting it for chopped parsley, coriander or tarragon.

SPICY SWEET POTATO LATKES

Unlike a fritter, which tends to be all about the egg, the focus of a latke is the potato – in this case, grated sweet potato, which is bound together with egg, flour and feta cheese, and flavoured with plenty of spice. They're a quick and easy breakfast alternative to toast or cereal, and taste great topped with sweet chilli yoghurt and fresh herbs.

MAKES ABOUT 10

1 large or 2 medium-sized sweet potatoes (500g), peeled and finely grated

2 eggs

60g feta cheese, crumbled

60g crispy fried onions (or chopped spring onions)

2 tbsp plain flour

1 tsp paprika

1 tsp dried chilli flakes

a generous pinch of salt and pepper

To serve:

1 tbsp sweet chilli sauce

a handful of fresh coriander, chopped

250g Greek yoghurt

PREP

Put a drizzle of olive oil in a large frying pan (big enough to fit all the latkes) and place it over a high heat on the hob. You'll also need a fish slice.

START THE CLOCK

Put the grated sweet potato in a sieve over the sink and squeeze it with a spoon to get rid of any excess moisture.

Leave it to drain while you mix together the rest of the latke ingredients. Then stir in the drained potato until the mixture comes together.

Shape the latkes into ten small, round patties, flattening them using the palm of your hand. Having slightly damp hands helps stop the mixture sticking to them.

When the oil is sizzling, arrange the latkes in the pan and fry for 2 minutes on each side, flipping them using the fish slice.

While they cook, make the garnish by stirring the sweet chilli sauce and coriander into the yoghurt. Don't mix it completely through – it looks nice if there's a swirl of sauce – and hold back some of the coriander for sprinkling on top of the latkes.

Serve hot, two or three per serving, drizzled with plenty of spiced yoghurt and herbs. Cooked, they should keep for 4 to 5 days in the fridge, or you can chill the uncooked latke mix for a week (or even freeze it for a month).

MASALA OMELETTE

Fed up of boring omelettes, I started putting flavours and spices – everything from sweet chilli sauce to cardamom (don't ask) – in mine in the morning. This masala-spiced one is the best of the lot, light and fluffy with a gentle chilli heat that will wake you and your taste buds up with a bang.

 SERVES 2 (OR 1 HUNGRY PERSON)

2 spring onions, finely chopped

1 red chilli, finely chopped

1 tomato, finely chopped

1½ tsp garam masala (an Indian spice made up of cumin, coriander, cinnamon, fennel and mace)

½ tsp turmeric (to give a lovely yellow colour)

a pinch of cayenne pepper (for heat)

a pinch each of salt and pepper

4 eggs

2 tbsp Greek yoghurt

To serve:

2 more tbsp Greek yoghurt

a few tsp mango chutney

a handful of coriander leaves

PREP

Drizzle a little vegetable oil (or a knob of butter, if you prefer) over the base of a large, non-stick frying pan and place it on the hob over a high heat. You'll also need a whisk, a palette knife and a fish slice.

—

 START THE CLOCK

Put the chopped veg into the hot pan. Mix the spices and seasoning together in a small bowl, add them to the pan and let this sauté away for 2 minutes until it's all softened and smells delicious.

While this cooks, crack the eggs into a bowl and stir in the yoghurt. Whisk until fully combined.

Tip the omelette mix into the hot pan and swirl it around so it completely covers the base. For the first minute of cooking, use a fork to jiggle it around a little bit – this ensures the heat is getting to the top layer of egg.

Cook the omelette on one side for 2 minutes. Now you can either flip it to the other side – by putting a plate on top, flipping the whole lot upside down and then sliding the omelette from the plate back into the pan – or use the palette knife and fish slice to fold one half on to the other. Alternatively you can fold both sides into the centre; it's your choice (depending whether you like the middle gooey or not).

Cook the omelette for a further minute before turning it out on to a plate.

Top with spoonfuls of Greek yoghurt, swirls of mango chutney and ripped coriander leaves. Dig in while it's hot.

CHAPTER 6:

party food

Wow your guests – whether there are six or sixty of them –
with these celebratory showstoppers, from fabulous
finger food to decadent cakes

Sloe gin jellies ◇ Mars bar spoon cake ◇ Pimped-up popcorn
◇ Halloumi fritters ◇ Nacho average cheesecake
◇ Peanut butter poke cake ◇ S'mores bites
◇ Flatbread pizzetta ◇ Festive nibbles tree ◇ Parmesan cups

SLOE GIN JELLIES

Just the ticket for warming the cockles (and raising the spirits) on a cold night, these pretty ruby-coloured jellies are sure to impress. They come with a health warning: they're seeeriously alcoholic, so if you want to swap some of the sloe gin for fruit juice or cordial, I won't hold it against you. Or if you want an extra kick, substitute Prosecco for soda water. Just don't say I didn't warn you . . .

 MAKES 4

150g fresh blackberries

4 leaves of gelatine

120ml sloe gin

60g granulated sugar

175ml soda water

175ml cranberry juice (you can also use apple and raspberry or red grape juice)

edible glitter, to decorate

 PREP

Wash and dry 4 serving glasses or dishes. I use champagne saucers, but you can also use ramekins – or, if you've got one, a large retro jelly mould (approx. 600ml) is perfect for this recipe.

 START THE CLOCK

First, arrange the blackberries in the base of your serving dishes and put them in the fridge to chill. This will speed up the setting process.

Put the gelatine leaves in a bowl of cold water to soften them up. Meanwhile, heat the sloe gin and sugar in a small saucepan over a low heat.

Once the sugar has dissolved, take the pan off the heat. Squeeze any excess water out of the gelatine leaves and add these to the gin mixture. Stir well to dissolve.

Add the soda water and cranberry juice and mix thoroughly. Decant the jelly into the serving dishes (don't worry if the blackberries float to the top) and dust the tops with edible glitter.

Put them in the fridge or a cold place to set for at least 3 hours.

Serve the jellies with shortbread on the side (trust me, you won't need any more gin). They'll keep for 4 to 5 days in the fridge.

MARS BAR SPOON CAKE

Stick this gooey, fudgey, chocolatey bowl of deliciousness in the middle of the table at parties and your guests will never want to go home. Give everyone a spoon – this is not the sort of cake you can daintily nibble with a fork – and tuck in while it's piping hot, topped with scoops of ice cream.

SERVES
4–6

100g unsalted butter

2 eggs

200g caster sugar

50g self-raising flour

40g cocoa powder

4 x small (40g) Mars bars, chopped into chunks

PREP

Grease a large Pyrex pie or flan dish (mine is 25cm across and 1.1-litre capacity) with a little butter or oil. I use a shallow dish rather than a cake tin as it helps the cake cook through – and also leaves more room for everyone to gather round and dig in!

You'll also need a whisk – electric, if you have one.

START THE CLOCK

Put the butter in a heatproof bowl and blast it on high in the microwave for around 20 to 30 seconds until it's melted.

Whisk the eggs and sugar until the mixture is pale and fluffy. Add the melted butter and whisk again to combine.

Sieve in the flour and cocoa powder and add two-thirds of the chopped Mars bars. Stir well.

Pour the cake mix into the prepared dish and spread it around so it covers the base. Arrange the remaining pieces of chopped Mars bar on top and press them into the mixture.

Microwave on high for 3 minutes, then carefully take it out and run a knife over the top of the cake – as if you're marbling icing – to spread the melted Mars bar around a little.

Microwave for another minute until it's cooked through. Watch out – the dish and the caramel from those Mars bars will be very hot, so leave it a few minutes before serving.

It's best eaten straight away for maximum gooiness but will keep for a few days in the fridge. Just blast it for another minute or so to remelt the chocolate.

PIMPED-UP POPCORN

Sweet or salted . . . which one are you? I like a mixture, but there are some days when plain old popcorn just won't do. The answer? My pimped-up popcorn, which takes the flavour combinations to a whole new level. Here are four twists on the simple snack . . .

 ALL RECIPES SERVE 4. For each, you'll need approximately 70g popped unsalted popcorn (I buy the microwave bags but you can make your own if you prefer).

Toasted coconut

50g desiccated coconut

40g coconut oil

25g unsalted butter

40g caster sugar

 **PREP**

Preheat the grill to high and put a small pan over a medium heat on the hob.

START THE CLOCK

Spread the desiccated coconut out on a baking tray and put it under the grill for a few minutes to toast. Keep an eye on it as it can turn from brown to black veeeery quickly!

Meanwhile, put the coconut oil, butter and sugar in a pan and melt until combined – it shouldn't take more than 4 minutes.

Tip the toasted coconut into the pan and stir it through. Pour this over the popcorn and mix thoroughly so every kernel is coated.

Caramel chai

20ml semi-skimmed milk

2 tsp instant chai drinking powder (available from most supermarkets)

80g shop-bought salted caramel sauce

PREP

Place a small saucepan over a medium heat on the hob.

START THE CLOCK

Put the milk and chai powder in the pan and stir until the chai has dissolved and the milk is bubbling.

Add the salted caramel and stir until the mixture is smooth.

Drizzle the hot sauce over the popcorn and serve immediately.

Truffle Parmesan

3 tsp truffle pesto (or you can use any other variety of pesto)

3 tsp olive oil

80g Parmesan cheese, grated

 PREP

Put a small pan over a medium heat on the hob.

 **START THE CLOCK**

Heat the pesto and olive oil in the pan – this loosens the pesto, making it go further, and also means the cheese will melt when it comes into contact with the hot sauce.

Drizzle the sauce over the popcorn, followed by the grated cheese, and mix thoroughly before serving.

Garlic and herb

60g salted butter

2 tsp garlic granules

1 tsp each of:
    dried or fresh thyme (chopped if fresh)
    dried or fresh rosemary (chopped)
    dried oregano

a few pinches of black pepper

 **PREP**

Place a small pan over a medium heat on the hob.

 **START THE CLOCK**

Melt the butter in the pan. When it starts to bubble and foam, add the garlic granules, herbs and pepper and mix thoroughly.

Pour this over the popcorn and stir it through. Serve warm.

HALLOUMI FRITTERS

If you, like me, just can't get enough halloumi cheese – that salty, moreish, crispy-on-the-outside, gooey-in-the-middle delight – then these fritters will put a massive smile on your face. Like chips but made of cheese, they're a cinch to make and a real crowd-pleaser.

**SERVES
8–10**

200ml sunflower or vegetable oil

2 x 250g blocks of halloumi

100g plain flour

2 tsp each of:
  ground cumin
  ground coriander
  mild paprika
  dried oregano

a few pinches of black pepper

To serve:

2 tbsp runny honey

a handful of pomegranate seeds

a handful of torn coriander
  leaves

PREP

In a large shallow frying pan (preferably one with a lid or splatter guard), pour the oil to cover the base and ½cm up the sides of the pan.

You'll know it's ready when it's bubbling and a crumb of bread (or halloumi) dropped into the oil sizzles and floats to the top of the pan. Have a slotted spoon to hand, and kitchen paper to soak up all that hot oil.

**START
THE CLOCK**

Lay the halloumi flat on a chopping board and slice it widthways (across the shortest length). Slice each half into five (along the longer length), and then cut each of these pieces into two. This should give you 20 'chip'-shaped slices of cheese from each block, so 40 fritters in total.

Mix the flour, spices, herbs and seasoning together in a small bowl. Then roll the cheese sticks in the spiced flour and carefully transfer to the hot oil. Let the fritters cook for 1 to 2 minutes on each side, until they're golden brown, and then flip on to the other side.

Transfer them on to a plate covered in kitchen paper so the oil can drain off.

Serve hot with honey, pomegranate seeds and fresh coriander.

TIP

It's great fun to experiment with the spices you use in the batter for these little halloumi fritters. Try cayenne pepper, paprika or ground chilli for an extra-hot twist, or za'atar – a Middle Eastern spice blend – for a fragrant, herby flavour.

NACHO AVERAGE CHEESECAKE

Excuse the pun, but I couldn't resist. All the best bits of a cheesecake, spread over sweet, crunchy 'nachos' – so you don't even need a spoon to dig in. I've gone for strawberries and white chocolate, but feel free to play around with flavour combinations. This one definitely has the wow factor.

SERVES 8–10

60g icing sugar

20g unsalted butter, melted

3 large white tortillas

100g white chocolate, 90g melted

250g mascarpone cheese

250g fresh strawberries, hulled and halved

1 tsp runny honey

 PREP

Preheat the oven to 250°C (fan 230°C) and cover a large baking sheet with tin foil (this will stop the nachos getting stuck). A hand blender will be useful, and you'll also need a nice big serving platter and a pastry brush.

 START THE CLOCK

Combine a tablespoon of icing sugar with the melted butter and brush this over the tortillas. Using scissors, cut them into eight triangles – just like slices of pizza.

Arrange the tortilla pieces on the baking sheet, butter side up, making sure there are no overlaps or they won't crisp up. Spread them out as much as possible. Bake them in the oven, on the top shelf, for 5 minutes.

Whisk 90g melted chocolate into the mascarpone and sieve in the remainder of the icing sugar. You should end up with a thick, smooth consistency.

Take a small handful of the prepared strawberries (40–50g) and purée them – either with a hand blender, if you have one, or by squishing them through a sieve with a fork. Mix the honey into the puréed strawberries to make a coulis.

Take the nachos out of the oven. Don't worry if they still seem a little soft, they will crisp up as they cool. Arrange them artfully on your serving platter, and top with dollops of cheesecake mix and swirls of strawberry coulis. Scatter the rest of the strawberries over the top.

Finish by grating the last 10g of white chocolate over the top.

This won't keep longer than a day – so no excuses! If you don't want to serve it straight away, keep the nachos in an airtight tin and the rest of the ingredients in the fridge, and assemble when you're ready to eat.

PEANUT BUTTER POKE CAKE

So called because you poke holes in the hot sponge and drizzle melted peanut butter over the top, this easy-peasy microwave cake is topped with crunchy, caramelized peanuts, and will have everyone coming back for seconds.

 MAKES 16 SMALL SQUARES

150g unsalted butter, softened

100g smooth peanut butter

150g caster sugar

100g Greek yoghurt

3 eggs

150g self-raising flour

For the caramelized nuts:

150g unsalted peanuts

60g caster sugar

1 tbsp unsalted butter

For the drizzle:

100g smooth peanut butter

5 tbsp water

 PREP

Grease a 20cm-square microwaveable baking dish (silicone, Pyrex or heatproof plastic) that can rotate fully in your microwave.

Put a frying pan on the hob over a high heat. You'll need a whisk, preferably electric, a wooden spoon for poking holes, and a small saucepan for the drizzle.

 START THE CLOCK

Whisk the butter, peanut butter, sugar, yoghurt and eggs together in a bowl. Sieve in the flour and stir to combine into a smooth batter.

Tip the batter into the prepared dish and microwave on high for approximately 5 minutes. You'll know it's done when the sponge is golden and risen.

While the cake bakes, caramelize the nuts. Roughly chop the peanuts and then add them to the hot frying pan with the sugar and butter. Mix sparingly – you want the sugar to catch and turn brown, enrobing the nuts in a lovely dark caramel.

For the drizzle, put the peanut butter in the small saucepan over a low heat and add the water. Stir as it melts and, once liquid, switch the heat off.

When the cake is ready, use the end of a wooden spoon to poke sixteen holes in the sponge, almost to the bottom. Drizzle the melted peanut butter over the top, making sure it fills the holes and spreads evenly over the sponge. Top the cake with the caramelized nuts. Slice into squares and serve, hot or cold. It should keep for 3 to 4 days in an airtight tin.

S'MORES BITES

Traditionally eaten round a campfire, s'mores originated in 1920s America and comprise a sort of biscuit 'sandwich' with a gooey, melted marshmallow and chocolate filling. The name comes from the phrase 'some more' – because once you've started eating them you'll want more and more . . . and more. My twist turns the childhood camping treat into a bite-sized party snack.

 MAKES 12

100g unsalted butter

14 digestive biscuits (approx. 220g)

24 squares milk chocolate (approx. 150g)

36 marshmallows (approx. 270g)

 PREP

Line a 12-hole muffin tray with paper cases and preheat the grill to its highest setting. You'll need a food processor (or a ziplock bag and rolling pin) to crush the biscuits.

 START THE CLOCK

Put the butter in a microwaveable bowl and melt it in the microwave on high, in bursts of 20 seconds. While it melts, blitz the digestives in the food processor, or put them in a ziplock bag and bash them with a rolling pin to turn them to crumbs.

Tip the biscuit crumbs into the melted butter and stir to combine. Divide the mixture between the 12 cases and press it down firmly with the back of a spoon so it's nicely compacted.

Place two squares of chocolate on top of each biscuit base, and top with three marshmallows.

Place the muffin tray under the grill, on the top oven shelf, for 3 minutes, until the marshmallows are golden and bubbling – just like they've been toasted over a campfire.

Leave the s'mores to cool a little before serving. They'll keep for a day or two if you can't eat them all at once.

FLATBREAD PIZZETTA

Made in a flash, on a flatbread or leftover tortilla wrap, this mini skinny pizzetta is ideal finger food for parties – or as a yummy dinner for one. I've kept my recipe veggie, with mozzarella and chargrilled veg, but you can add whatever toppings you want.

 MAKES 1 (SERVES 1 AS A MEAL OR 4 AS FINGER FOOD)

2 tbsp shop-bought pesto

1 large flatbread or tortilla (you can also use naan bread)

125g ball of mozzarella

180g pot of roasted mixed veg (I use chargrilled peppers, tomatoes and courgette)

a handful of fresh rocket

a generous grind of black pepper

 PREP

Put a knob of butter in a large ovenproof frying pan – with a circumference big enough to fit the whole flatbread – and put it on the hob over a high heat. You're ready to start once the butter is melted and sizzling. You'll also need to preheat the grill to high.

 START THE CLOCK

Spread 1 tbsp pesto over the flatbread and place it, pesto side up, in the hot pan.

Slice the mozzarella and arrange this over the flatbread, along with slices of mixed veg. Dot the remaining 1 tbsp pesto over the top, followed by the black pepper.

Leave the pizzetta to cook in the pan for a minute or so until it starts sizzling.

Transfer the frying pan to the grill, placing it on the highest oven shelf. Let the pizzetta cook for a further 4 minutes, until the cheese is melted and the flatbread is crisp and golden around the edges.

Serve topped with the fresh rocket. It's best eaten on the day it's made, but the pizzetta can be reheated (by placing it under the grill for another few minutes) if you want to make it ahead and crisp it up later.

 TIP

Experiment with different flavours of pesto (sun-dried tomato or red pepper pesto work well) and toppings: sliced mushrooms, heritage tomatoes, spinach, Parmesan and Parma ham are all classics. You could even make a sweet version by slathering the flatbread with chocolate spread or peanut butter instead of pesto and topping it with fresh fruit.

FESTIVE NIBBLES TREE

I love having people over to my house around Christmas: sparkly jumpers, mince pies and the scent of mulled wine wafting from the kitchen. But guests need nibbles – and this cheese-based festive treat is the perfect showstopper to impress, without much effort. If you want to make it at another time of year, simply mould the base into a dome, ball or shape of your choice.

SERVES 8–10

4 x 150g packets of hard cream cheese (e.g. Boursin or French Roulé)

1 x 280g packet of spreadable cream cheese

a handful of chopped parsley

1 tsp each of:
dried onion powder
chilli flakes
ground black pepper

To decorate the tree:

2 x 150g punnets of green olives

200g punnet of mixed antipasti (black olives, sun-dried tomatoes, peppers and artichokes)

optional: small piece of fresh yellow pepper, chilli or Cheddar

selection of crackers, breads and cured meats

 PREP

 START THE CLOCK

Roll out two large sheets of cling film and place one over a large chopping board.

In a big bowl, mix together the two cheeses, parsley and all the seasoning.

Tip the cheese mixture on to the sheet of cling film on the chopping board, making sure you pile it nice and high. Place the other sheet over the top and use it to protect your hands as you mould the cheese into a conical tree shape. The taller the better, so it's not too dense.

Once you're happy with the shape, transfer the cheese tree to your serving plate. Remove the bottom sheet of cling film first, and hold the tree carefully by the top one as you move it over. You can smooth the sides or make it slightly taller with a knife.

Now it's time to start decorating with antipasti 'baubles'. You can be neat and symmetrical or completely random (they say you can tell a lot about a person by the way they decorate their tree). Stick green olives all over, pushing them in just enough so they stay in place. You can use cocktail sticks to secure them, if you need to.

Wedge tomatoes, artichokes and red peppers in the gaps between the olives. Keep going until the tree is completely covered and you can no longer see the cheese.

I like to use chargrilled yellow pepper as the 'star' on the top, but feel free to let your imagination run wild: you can cut a star shape out of a fresh pepper or chilli or even a piece of Cheddar.

Arrange crackers, breads, cured meats and anything else that takes your fancy on the plate around the base of the tree.

Keep it in the fridge so it holds its shape until you're ready to serve. The tree will keep for 2 days but is best eaten on the day it's made.

PARMESAN CUPS

These easy cheesy canapés have just one main ingredient: Parmesan cheese, which melts and bubbles until it's golden and then forms the base of these crisp pleated cups. You can fill them with whatever you want: my favourite is described below but feel free to let your imagination run wild.

 MAKES 8

300g Parmesan, finely grated

1 tbsp plain flour

a few grinds of coarse
    black pepper

For the filling:

250g heirloom tomatoes (the
    little multicoloured ones)

a handful of parsley

2 tbsp olive oil

juice of 1 lemon

salt and pepper

 PREP

Preheat the oven to 220°C (fan 200°C). Line a baking sheet with greaseproof paper and clean and dry the underside of a 12-hole muffin tray.

You'll also need an 8cm round pastry cutter (or you can use the base of a mug), and a fish slice will come in handy.

 START THE CLOCK

Mix the cheese and flour together and divide into eight portions.

Tip each one in turn into the round cutter on the baking sheet, pressing the cheese down with your fingertips so it holds the circular shape. (If you're using a mug, you'll have to draw around the rim on the greaseproof paper and then keep the cheese within the lines.) Make sure to space the circles out as they'll spread slightly as they cook.

Grind some pepper over each one. Bake for 4 minutes, until the cheese is melted and bubbling.

While they cook, make the filling. Cut the tomatoes into quarters and finely chop the parsley. Put them in a bowl and drizzle over the olive oil, lemon juice and seasoning. Toss to combine and set aside.

When the cups are ready, invert the muffin tray so it's upside down, with the curved muffin bases pointing upwards. Working quickly, roughly cut out the greaseproof paper around the circles of melted cheese.

Flip each one upside down – use a fish slice if you need to as there may be excess hot oil – on to an inverted muffin base, so the greaseproof paper is uppermost and the cheese is in direct contact with the tray.

Gently press the edges of each cheesy cup down and in, so it detaches from the greaseproof paper and takes on the shape of the muffin case. Leave for a few minutes to cool and crisp up before filling with spoonfuls of the tomato mixture.

If you're filling them straight away, eat the cups on the same day. Unfilled, they'll keep for 2 to 3 days in an airtight tin, though they may start to lose their crispness.

 TIP   *Other filling ideas include: Caesar salad (cooked chicken, bacon, lettuce and Caesar dressing), sautéed leeks and mushrooms, or chopped steamed spinach with garlic and sea salt.*

CHAPTER 7:

fruity favourites

From stuffed apples to sticky rum skewers,

banana blondies to cupcakes made with Pimm's,

these fruity treats will become firm favourites

Spiced figs with mascarpone cream ◇ Tropical coconut whip

◇ Toasty ginger cobbler ◇ Pimm's cupcakes ◇ Banana blondies

◇ Fig roll ◇ Griddled peach crunch ◇ Frosted berries with hot choc sauce

◇ Stewed apple with yoghurt custard ◇ Rum pineapple skewers

SPICED FIGS with MASCARPONE CREAM

Rich, jammy and ever so stylish, figs are perfect fodder for a showstopping dessert – and you can make this one in record time. Honey and mixed spice are classic accompaniments to these juicy Asian fruits, while the cool whipped mascarpone is a lovely contrast to all that sweetness.

 SERVES 4

8 large ripe figs (approx. 440g)

25g unsalted butter, softened

2 tsp mixed spice

5 tbsp runny honey

60g shelled pistachios, roughly chopped

For the mascarpone cream:

200ml whipping cream

½ tsp vanilla extract

50g icing sugar

150g mascarpone cheese, softened

 PREP

Preheat the grill to medium-high and line a large baking sheet with tin foil. An electric whisk will be useful, if you have one.

 START THE CLOCK

Arrange the figs on the baking sheet. Cut a deep cross in the top of each one and press the quarters downwards so they fan out like the petals of a flower.

Use a teaspoon to drop a small knob of butter into the centre of each fig. Stir the mixed spice through the honey and then drizzle this over the top. Finish with a sprinkling of nuts.

Grill for 5 minutes, until the figs are soft and sizzling in their sticky spiced sauce.

While they cook, make the mascarpone cream. Put the cream and vanilla extract in a bowl and sieve in the icing sugar. Using the whisk, beat the mixture on high speed until soft peaks form. Add the mascarpone and whisk for another minute until it thickens.

Serve the figs hot, two per person, with a generous helping of pillowy cream on the side. If you don't want to eat them straight away, both parts will keep, well covered, in the fridge for a couple of days.

TROPICAL COCONUT WHIP

This dairy-free dessert is sweet, refreshing and toooootally tropical. Coconut cream is such a versatile ingredient – not only does it have the bubbly consistency of whipped cream but it's got a lovely fresh flavour, and it's good for you, too.

 SERVES 2

2 fresh mangoes, peeled and chopped into chunks

3 fresh passion fruits, seeds and juice decanted

juice of 1 lemon

130g chilled coconut cream – you only want the firmer stuff from the top of the tin, not the juice underneath, so to get this

amount I use 2 x 160g tins of supermarket coconut cream

40g icing sugar

300g fresh tropical fruit, chopped into chunks (I use a shop-bought pot containing coconut, papaya, watermelon and melon)

30g pistachios, shelled and chopped

 PREP

You'll need two large serving glasses or dishes. I use gin tumblers, which have a capacity of 300ml. Whatever you choose, make sure they're transparent so you can appreciate the layers.

Put a small saucepan over a medium heat on the hob. You'll also need an electric whisk, if you have one to hand.

 START THE CLOCK

Put the mangoes, passion fruit seeds and juice and lemon juice in the saucepan and leave them to stew down into a fruity compote.

Meanwhile, scrape the coconut cream out of the tins and into a large bowl. Use a spoon to break it up a little, sieve in the icing sugar, and then whisk it for 3 to 4 minutes until it's light and fluffy.

Now it's time to assemble the desserts. First, put a layer of chopped tropical fruit in each glass. Top with the whipped coconut cream and then a layer of compote.

Repeat this in at least two layers. Finally, top with any remaining tropical fruit and scatter the pistachio nuts over the top.

Dig in straight away. Assembled, they'll keep for a couple of days in the fridge – or you can keep the unassembled ingredients fresh for up to a week.

 TIP

Don't throw out the coconut milk that's left in the tins once you've scraped out the creamy top – save it to use in curries, as a salad dressing or in smoothies.

TOASTY GINGER COBBLER

A super-simple dessert that will impress your guests without any stress behind the scenes, my toasty ginger cobbler is made from fresh fruit, crunchy cereal topping and a zingy ginger compote, which you'll find alongside the jam in most supermarkets. Serve hot on a chilly evening.

 SERVES 4

2 apples, peeled, cored and thinly sliced

100g fresh raspberries

4 tbsp ginger compote

4 tbsp warm water

180g crunchy granola (I use Jordan's Country Crisp but any variety will do)

 PREP

You'll need a small, round (approx. 20cm diameter) microwave-safe and heat-proof dish or cake tin. Preheat the grill to high and place a baking sheet on the top shelf.

 START THE CLOCK

Lay the sliced apple over the base of the dish and scatter the raspberries over the top.

In a small bowl, mix the ginger compote with the water and spoon this evenly over the fruit layer. Place the dish in the microwave and heat on high for 3 minutes.

Remove the dish, spread the cereal over the top of the fruit and put it on the baking sheet under the grill for another 2 minutes, until the topping is crisp and golden.

Serve sizzling, with generous scoops of ice cream or whipped cream. If you don't eat it all in one sitting, it'll keep in the fridge for 2 to 3 days.

 TIP

This is a great dish to experiment with. Try making it with different types of fruit, cereal or compote: I like morello cherry, blackberry jam or tart apple compote. You can also try drained tinned fruit rather than fresh, such as black cherries, rhubarb or halved pears.

PIMM'S CUPCAKES

A bite of these fluffy, fruity cupcakes is like a mouthful of summer. The bubbles in the Pimm's act as a raising agent, working together with the self-raising flour to make the sponge light and airy like a fairy cake – the perfect post-BBQ treat for grown-ups.

MAKES 12

125g unsalted butter, softened

150g golden caster sugar

3 eggs

60ml ready-mixed Pimm's

zest of 1 lemon

zest of 1 orange

150g self-raising flour, sifted

For the icing/decoration:

30g unsalted butter, softened

200g icing sugar

25ml ready-mixed Pimm's

6 strawberries, halved

12 sprigs of fresh mint

PREP

You'll need twelve silicone cupcake moulds (better than paper as they hold their shape when cooking) and a flat, microwaveable plate to bake them on. An electric whisk is good, if you have one, and a piping bag or sandwich bag with a small hole (approx. 1cm) snipped in one corner is needed for icing the cupcakes.

START THE CLOCK

Beat the butter and sugar together, using the whisk.

In a separate bowl, loosely beat the eggs with the Pimm's and citrus zest.

Add half the egg mixture along with half the flour to the butter and sugar, and combine fully before adding the other half.

Divide half the batter between six cupcake cases, spaced out on the microwave-proof plate. Don't fill them too much – a heaped tablespoon in each is enough – or they'll overflow as they bake.

Bake for 2 minutes on high, then repeat with the other six. The cakes should rise in domes to the tops of the cases and turn golden when they're done.

While the cupcakes bake, make the icing. Whisk the butter, icing sugar and Pimm's together to make a light, fluffy buttercream. Allow the cakes to cool slightly before piping mounds of buttercream on top of each and finishing with half a strawberry and a sprig of mint.

Serve immediately – with a tall glass of Pimm's (you don't want any going to waste, after all). They'll keep for 2 to 3 days in an airtight container.

BANANA BLONDIES

Squidgy, indulgent and studded with white chocolate chips, these are the ultimate comfort food. Blondies are, in my humble opinion, even better than brownies; without the chocolate you can really taste the buttery sponge, while the brown sugar tastes rich and caramelly.

 MAKES 20

100g unsalted butter

2 eggs

2 tbsp semi-skimmed milk

2 ripe bananas, peeled and mashed

120g self-raising flour, sifted

2 tsp ground cinnamon

1 tsp mixed spice

100g dark brown sugar

100g white chocolate chips

 PREP

Grease a square, microwave-proof baking dish (silicone or Pyrex, approx. 20cm x 20cm) with a little butter or flavourless oil.

—

 START THE CLOCK

Put the butter into a heatproof dish, cover with a sheet of kitchen paper and melt it in the microwave. Do it on high in 20-second bursts so it doesn't burn or spit all over the inside of your microwave – it shouldn't take longer than 40 seconds.

Crack in the eggs, add the milk and mashed bananas, and stir to combine.

Next, put the flour into a separate bowl and stir in the spices and sugar. Add the melted butter and banana mixture to this and mix well. Stir through half the chocolate chips.

Tip the blondie batter into the baking dish and spread it to the edges. Scatter the remaining chocolate chips on top.

Microwave on high for 4.5 minutes. Keep an eye on it – you may need to rotate the dish halfway through if it looks like it's cooking unevenly – and don't overbake or it will dry out.

Leave to cool completely in the dish before slicing into squares. The blondies will keep for 3 to 4 days in an airtight tin.

 TIP

—

You could make banoffee blondies by substituting half the chocolate chips for chunks of chewy toffee or fudge. Or try adding 50g chopped walnuts to the batter for a nutty banana traybake.

FIG ROLL

A traditional fig-stuffed sweet roll this is not, so look elsewhere if you're desperate to recreate those moreish biscuits of your childhood. Instead, my six-minute fig roll is a sticky, savoury treat: one to slice and eat with cheese or spread on a hunk of crusty bread and enjoy with a slab of Brie.

 SERVES 8–10

270g dried figs, roughly chopped (make sure you cut off the hard stalks)

50g blanched whole almonds

90g dried apricots

40g walnut pieces

1 tbsp runny honey

a pinch of nutmeg

a pinch of ground cinnamon

 PREP

Preheat the grill to high. Prepare a large sheet of greaseproof paper for wrapping the roll, along with two pieces of string or elastic bands to secure the ends. A food processor will be very useful for this recipe.

 START THE CLOCK

Whiz the figs in the food processor until they come together into a big, sticky ball (or finely chop them if you're doing it by hand).

While these are being blitzed, spread the almonds on a baking sheet and stick them under the grill for 3 minutes until lightly toasted. Chop the apricots and walnuts finely using a sharp knife.

Next, decant the figs into a large bowl with the apricots and walnuts, and put the almonds into the food processor. Blitz until they're ground into chunks (or bash them with a rolling pin).

Add these to the bowl, along with the honey and spices, and stir until it's all combined.

Transfer the mixture to the greaseproof paper, fold a layer over the top and roll it into a tightly packed cylinder, 5 to 6cm in diameter. Flatten the ends of the paper, fold them inwards and secure each end with string or a rubber band.

Put the roll in the fridge for 2 to 3 hours until it's solidified. Unwrap as required and slice into 1cm rounds. Chilled, it should keep for up to a month.

GRIDDLED PEACH CRUNCH

Peaches, to me, are the sunshine fruit. They're packed full of vitamin C, so they're incredibly good for you, and there's nothing better than biting into a chilled, juicy peach on a summery day. Here, I've created a pretty platter that ensures these succulent beauties are the centre of attention.

 SERVES 8–10

6 peaches or nectarines

1 tbsp olive oil

75g your favourite crunchy granola

2 tbsp runny honey

zest and juice of ½ an orange

160g Greek yoghurt

a handful of mint leaves

a handful of pomegranate seeds

 PREP

I like to serve this on a huge platter, right in the middle of the table, and you'll need a pastry brush for brushing oil on the peaches.

You'll also need to have two hobs on high – one for a griddle pan (make sure this is dry, with no oil or water residue) and one for a small saucepan. Preheat the oven to 160°C (fan 140°C).

 START THE CLOCK

Slice the peaches into thin segments and brush these with the olive oil. When the griddle pan is smoking hot, lay the segments in it. You should hear them start to sizzle immediately.

Meanwhile, spread the granola out on a baking tray and put it in the oven for 3 minutes.

Put the honey and orange zest and juice into the saucepan and stir. The mixture should blend together and start to bubble – when it does, switch the heat off.

Once the peaches have been griddled for a few minutes, flip the segments over to the other side and let them cook for another few minutes.

Now it's time to assemble your showstopper. First, arrange the peaches on the plate. Next, dollop generous spoonfuls of Greek yoghurt all over, followed by a sprinkling of granola, and then pour over your sauce. Finish with the mint leaves, gently torn so they start to release their flavour, and a scattering of pomegranate seeds.

Serve in the centre of the table so everyone can help themselves. This doesn't keep, so there's every excuse for second helpings.

FROSTED BERRIES with HOT CHOC SAUCE

This is my take on a fruity dessert I first tried at a restaurant . . . although my mum swears she made it for me when I was little, too. It's all about the combination of textures, flavours and temperatures: tangy, ice-cold berries sparkling with frost; rich, creamy hot chocolate sauce – it's a match made in heaven when the sauce hits the berries and they release their gorgeous purple juices.

 SERVES 4

500g mixed frozen berries (strawberries, raspberries, blackberries, cherries . . . any variety will do)

170ml double cream

100g white chocolate

optional: 1 vanilla pod

a few sprigs of mint

zest of ½ an orange

 PREP

Clean and dry your serving dishes. I like to serve this in one big bowl in the middle of the table so everyone can dig in, but you can use individual dessert bowls or plates if you prefer. Put a small saucepan over a medium heat on the hob.

 START THE CLOCK

Remove the berries from the freezer and decant them into the bowl(s). They'll need around 6 minutes to just lose their frozen hardness, so this is perfect timing.

Pour the cream into the saucepan and add the chocolate, broken into pieces. If you're using a vanilla pod, split this in half lengthways, scoop out the seeds and add them at this stage. Stir gently for 4 to 5 minutes until the chocolate has melted and the sauce is smooth.

Pour the sauce into a warmed jug (I fill mine with boiling water first to heat it up) and serve alongside the defrosting berries, scattered with a few sprigs of mint and a sprinkling of orange zest.

It needs to be eaten straight away, but chances are that won't be a problem! You're more likely to end up fighting over who gets to lick the bowl . . .

STEWED APPLE with YOGHURT CUSTARD

This autumnal dish makes a delicious dessert – or a hearty breakfast – and has become a firm favourite in my house. Using yoghurt to make the custard keeps it light and healthy, while the stewed apples are stuffed full of caramelized nuts and spices.

 SERVES 2

2 small cooking apples, cored but unpeeled

½ tbsp sultanas

½ tbsp finely chopped nuts

1 tsp soft light brown sugar

1 tsp cinnamon

a pinch of nutmeg

4 tbsp water

For the custard:

2 egg yolks

150ml Greek yoghurt

3 tsp runny honey

 PREP

You'll need a shallow microwaveable bowl or dish big enough to fit both apples. Grease this with a little butter so they don't get stuck as they bake.

Put a small saucepan on the hob over a medium heat.

 START THE CLOCK

Pierce the apple skins in several places using a fork or a cocktail stick, if you have one handy (this allows the steam to escape and stops them getting too hot).

In a small bowl, mix together the sultanas, nuts, sugar and spices. Arrange the apples in the prepared dish and carefully spoon the mixture into the centre (where the core was).

Squeeze in as much as you can but don't worry if there's some left over. Put this in the bottom of the dish along with the water – this makes a tasty little sauce to add to the custard.

Microwave the apples on high for 5 minutes.

While they bake, put all the ingredients for the custard in the saucepan. Stir continuously until the mixture boils and thickens (turn the heat up if you need to) – and then take it off the heat. This should take around 4 to 5 minutes.

Spoon the excess sauce over the apples and serve straight away, with plenty of hot custard on the side.

RUM PINEAPPLE SKEWERS

Rum-infused caramel sauce is the secret to this fruity dessert. The pineapple wedges are griddled in a dry pan (or, if you prefer, over a hot barbecue), giving them lovely charred edges, and then drenched in this sweet, sticky, spicy sauce, the perfect contrast to the tropical fruit.

 SERVES 4

½ a pineapple (approx. 500g), sliced into 12 long wedges

30ml spiced rum

100g shop-bought caramel sauce

50g unsalted butter

a pinch of salt

 PREP

You'll need twelve wooden skewers, soaked in cold water before cooking so they don't burn. Put a dry griddle pan over a high heat on the hob, and a smaller saucepan over a medium heat.

 START THE CLOCK

Thread the pineapple wedges lengthways on to the skewers and arrange them in the hot griddle pan. You'll know the temperature's right if they sizzle straight away; keep an eye on them and turn them every minute so they don't burn.

Pour the rum into the other saucepan and heat it for a minute so the alcohol cooks off. Add the caramel sauce, butter and salt and stir until combined.

As it cooks, the sauce will bubble up and thicken. Keep stirring so it doesn't stick.

When the pineapple is griddled all over (approx. 5 minutes), arrange three skewers per person on a plate, and drizzle with plenty of caramel sauce. Serve any remaining sauce in a jug on the side.

The skewers can be reheated by putting them back in the griddle pan, if you don't eat them straight away. Both the fruit and the sauce will keep, well covered, for up to 3 days in the fridge.

CHAPTER 8:

iced desserts

To keep you cool on a hot summer's day, or to cosy up with on a winter's night, these iced desserts are perfect for kids and big kids alike

Frozen Nutella loaf ◇ Coco ice lollies ◇ Mango passion fruit ice ◇ Sunshine smoothie lollies ◇ Elderflower semifreddo ◇ Instant sorbet ◇ Ginger berry pops ◇ Baileys cheesecake ◇ Lemon meringue ice cream ◇ Freezer bag ice cream ◇ Cinnamon bun bombe

FROZEN NUTELLA LOAF

I'm a Nutella addict, so anything that involves the chocolate hazelnut spread is a winner in my book. Like a cheesecake but made in a loaf tin, this easy layered dessert looks impressive – and tastes utterly delicious. Better still, you can make it weeks ahead of time and keep it on ice.

 **SERVES
8–10**

1 x 400g tub Nutella	400g cream cheese
50g unsalted butter	80g icing sugar, sifted
200g Hobnobs (13–14 biscuits)	50g chopped roasted hazelnuts

 PREP

Line a standard loaf tin (approx. 2lb or 1 litre) with cling film, completely covering the base and sides and making sure there's plenty of excess overlapping the edges. I use three strips – one for each long side and one for the middle. Place a medium saucepan on the hob and turn the heat up high. You'll also need a food processor (or a ziplock bag and a rolling pin) for crushing the biscuits, and a whisk.

**START
THE CLOCK**

Put 150g Nutella and the butter in the pan and melt, stirring often so they don't burn.

Meanwhile, blitz the biscuits in the food processor until they turn to crumbs, or you can put them in a ziplock bag and bash them with a rolling pin.

When the mixture in the pan has melted to a smooth chocolate paste, tip the biscuit crumbs into the pan and stir until combined. Pour this into the lined loaf tin and use the back of a spoon to press it down.

In a separate bowl, whisk the remaining Nutella with the cream cheese and sifted icing sugar until smooth. Tip this into the loaf tin and spread on top of the biscuit base.

Finish with the chopped hazelnuts, covering the surface right to the edges. Wrap the excess cling film over the top of the loaf to cover it and place in the freezer for 3 to 4 hours to set.

Remove from the freezer around 20 minutes before serving and slice with a sharp knife dipped in boiling water. If you don't eat it all in one go, keep the rest of the loaf, well covered, in the freezer – it should last for 2 to 3 months.

COCO ICE LOLLIES

These little lollies are made from coconut water, so they're incredibly refreshing – and not bad for you either. The slices of suspended fruit in your lolly look lovely, while the zingy combination of fresh mint and pink peppercorns gives them a sophisticated kick.

 MAKES 4

2 kiwis

½ a large orange

1 tbsp maple syrup

1 tsp pink peppercorns

a handful of fresh mint leaves, torn

200ml coconut water

 PREP

Clean and dry four lolly moulds and lids/sticks.

———

 START THE CLOCK

Peel and slice the kiwis. Peel and deseed/de-pith the orange half and cut the flesh into small chunks.

Transfer the fruit to a small bowl and add the maple syrup, peppercorns and mint leaves. Stir to combine and leave it to macerate for a few minutes.

Pour the coconut water into the lolly moulds, filling each one around halfway full.

Divide the fruit mixture between the moulds, making sure the good bits get evenly distributed right down to the bottom of the moulds.

Put the lids on and freeze the lollies for at least 4 hours before serving.

They'll keep in the freezer for up to a month.

———

 TIP

Run the moulds under hot water from the tap for a minute to loosen them before pulling the lollies out. And feel free to experiment with different fruits: berries work well, as do slices of melon, watermelon, mango or cherry. You could also add 1 tbsp of popping candy for an extra kick.

MANGO PASSION FRUIT ICE

This frozen fruity concoction combines all my favourite summery flavours in a creamy dessert. Tropical mango and passion fruit work so well together, while the addition of lime juice adds a refreshing zing and stops it all being too sweet.

 SERVES 6–8

2 large fresh mangoes (approx. 350g), peeled and roughly chopped

450ml double or whipping cream

1 x 397g tin of condensed milk

2 tsp fresh lime juice

3 fresh passion fruit, seeds and juice decanted

 PREP

You'll need a 1-litre freezer-proof Tupperware container (or standard loaf tin). To make it easier to clean and get the ice cream out, I line mine with cling film (one strip for each long side and a strip for the middle), but you don't have to do this. A food processor will be useful here, and you'll need a hand whisk.

 START THE CLOCK

Put the mango into the food processor and whiz on high until it's puréed and there are only a few lumps left.

While this is being blitzed, whisk the cream until it forms soft peaks. It should only take a minute – don't over-whip it or it will turn to 'summer butter' (lumpy and not very nice).

Stir the condensed milk into the whipped cream, followed by the lime juice. Finally, add the puréed mango and the passion fruit juice and seeds. Stir thoroughly until combined.

Pour the ice cream mix into the prepared tin and leave it to freeze for 5 to 6 hours. Serve slightly defrosted, in generous scoops, as a deliciously cooling dessert.

It should keep in the freezer for 2 to 3 months.

SUNSHINE SMOOTHIE LOLLIES

This recipe uses all the ingredients from my favourite smoothie: a spicy blend of carrot, apple, orange, ginger and turmeric, a vibrant yellow spice grown in India and Indonesia. It gives a real kick – and turning it into lolly form makes this the ultimate refreshing pick-me-up.

 MAKES 4

2 carrots (approx. 300g), peeled and roughly chopped

25g fresh ginger, peeled and chopped into small pieces

2 apples (approx. 300g), peeled, cored and roughly chopped

1 tsp ground turmeric

300ml fresh orange juice

 PREP

You'll need four lolly moulds and sticks, so make sure these are washed and dried beforehand. You'll also need a food processor or blender, a sieve and a large jug.

 START THE CLOCK

Put all the ingredients, minus the orange juice, into the food processor and pulse on high for 3 minutes until they're puréed and nearly smooth.

Add two-thirds of the orange juice and pulse for another minute, until it makes a thick liquid.

Suspend the sieve over the jug and tip the mixture from the blender into the sieve. This will get rid of any pulp, skin or pips and give you a lovely smooth lolly base.

Finally, top up with the remaining orange juice and pour the liquid into the lolly moulds.

Freeze for at least 4 hours until firmly set. To remove from the moulds, pop them under the hot tap for a few seconds on each side and gently slide the lollies out.

They should keep for up to 3 months in the freezer.

ELDERFLOWER SEMIFREDDO

'Semifreddo' means 'half-frozen' and this tasty iced dessert has the consistency of a frozen mousse, thanks to the whipped egg yolks and lashings of cream. I've combined two of my favourite flavours – elderflower and white chocolate – which give it a sweet but also refreshing flavour.

**SERVES
10–12**

3 egg yolks

150g caster sugar

85ml elderflower cordial

1 tsp vanilla extract

250ml double or whipping cream

200g crème fraîche

80g white chocolate, melted

 PREP

Line a 1-litre freezer-proof container or loaf tin with cling film, ensuring there's plenty of overlap (so you can wrap it over the top of the semifreddo – I use one strip for each of the long sides and one for the middle). Put a mixing bowl in the freezer to chill.

Place a small saucepan on the hob over a medium heat. You'll also need a whisk – electric, if you have one.

 **START
THE CLOCK**

Put the egg yolks, sugar, elderflower cordial and vanilla extract in the saucepan and stir for a minute or so until the mixture starts to thicken and turn pale.

Transfer it to the cold bowl and whisk until it reaches the consistency of thick custard.

In a separate bowl, whisk the cream with the crème fraîche until it makes soft peaks. Make sure the white chocolate is cooled before adding it and stirring to combine.

A little at a time, add the egg mixture to the cream mixture, stirring constantly to ensure there are no lumps.

Pour the semifreddo mix into the prepared tin and transfer it to the freezer. Chill for at least 5 to 6 hours.

Defrost for around 15 minutes before serving it in slices, topped, if you want, with fresh red fruit and a drizzle of elderflower cordial.

It should keep in the freezer, well covered, for up to 2 months.

INSTANT SORBET

This is one of the simplest recipes in the world – just three ingredients, six minutes and you'll have a showstopping sorbet to rival the best gelaterias. I always keep a bag of frozen berries in my freezer for this recipe – you can buy them from the supermarket or chop up your favourite fruits and make your own. It's a great way to preserve them when they're about to go off.

 SERVES 4

300g frozen mixed berries (I use raspberries, blackberries, blackcurrants, redcurrants and strawberries)

2 tbsp maple syrup

100ml fruit cordial of your choice, made up according to the instructions

To serve:

a few sprigs of mint

a handful of fresh berries

 PREP

Take the berries out of the freezer to soften up around 10 minutes before you want to make the sorbet. You'll also need a food processor or blender; a hand blender will do.

 START THE CLOCK

Put the berries in the food processor and give them a blast for a minute or two, just to break up the ice.

Add the maple syrup and fruit cordial and whiz until you have a smooth, rich purple sorbet.

Scoop it out and serve immediately, garnished, if you want, with sprigs of mint and fresh berries.

You can refreeze this if you don't eat it all straight away (it'll keep in the freezer for 2 to 3 months), but it will need a good half an hour to defrost to get back to that lovely sorbet consistency.

 TIP

Try swapping the fruit cordial for an adult alternative: champagne diluted with elderflower cordial; Campari or Framboise with soda water; or even yoghurt or clotted cream if you fancy a creamier sorbet. Just make it all up to 100ml/100g so it doesn't overpower the fruit.

GINGER BERRY POPS

Half-smoothie, half-cheesecake, these healthy(ish) frozen yoghurt pops are a great treat – and kids will love them. The zingy ginger nut tops give a lovely crunch, and I love how the purple berries make the yoghurt look like it's been tie-dyed.

 MAKES 6

100g ginger nut biscuits (approx. 10)

1 x 397g tin of condensed milk

200g frozen mixed berries

200g Greek yoghurt

1 tsp ground ginger

 PREP

You'll need six paper cups or wide cylindrical lolly moulds, plus six sticks (or wooden skewers snapped in half). Take the berries out of the freezer 10 minutes before you start so they're a little defrosted.

A food processor will come in handy for crushing the biscuits and blitzing the fruit.

 START THE CLOCK

Either blitz the biscuits in a food processor or put them in a ziplock bag and bash them on a chopping board with a rolling pin until they turn to crumbs.

Tip the biscuit crumbs into a bowl and add 2 tbsp condensed milk. Mix until it starts to come together. Divide this between the paper cups/lolly moulds, using a teaspoon to press down and compact the biscuit mix.

Blitz the berries in the food processor (or mash them in a bowl if this is easier). You want them to be in small pieces but not puréed, with plenty of bigger chunks left.

In a large bowl, mix the berries with the yoghurt, ginger and the rest of the condensed milk. Stir gently – as the berries defrost, they'll create lovely purple streaks through the yoghurt, and you want to leave it partly mixed so it's not all one colour.

Decant the berry mixture into the paper cups/lolly moulds, on top of the ginger base, smoothing it down as you go. It should fill them around two-thirds of the way to the top.

Put the sticks into the centre of each lolly, pressing them down so they go into the biscuit base (this will help them stand up).

Freeze for at least 3 hours before serving. They'll keep for around a month in the freezer.

BAILEYS CHEESECAKE

Whether it's served in a chilled glass, swirled into hot chocolate or baked in a cake, I'm a sucker for Baileys – so much so that sometimes I need reminding it's alcoholic, as I could glug it at all hours of the day. My frozen cheesecake celebrates the creamy chocolate liqueur by making it the centrepiece of this fabulous dessert.

**SERVES
8–10**

250g milk chocolate digestives
(approx. 15)

100g unsalted butter, melted

500g full-fat cream cheese

100g icing sugar

2 tbsp Baileys or other cream
liqueur

300ml double or whipping cream

100g dark chocolate, 90g
chopped into small chunks

PREP

Grease and line a 20cm-round cake tin (springform is best – the ones with clip-together sides that come away from the base) with greaseproof paper. You'll also need a rolling pin, an electric whisk, if you have one, and a potato peeler or grater for curling the chocolate.

—

**START
THE CLOCK**

Put the biscuits in a large bowl and bash them with the end of a rolling pin until they turn to crumbs – a few larger chunks are fine. (You can also do this in a food processor, or place in a ziplock bag before bashing to prevent mess.)

Add the melted butter and stir until the mixture has the consistency of wet sand. Tip this into the base of the tin and press it down, then chill in the freezer.

Put the cream cheese in a bowl and lightly whip it until it's smooth. Sieve in the icing sugar, add the Baileys and stir until combined.

In a separate bowl, whip the cream to soft peaks using the electric whisk. Fold this into the cream cheese mixture, then mix in the 90g chopped chocolate.

Scrape the cheesecake topping on to the chilled biscuit base. Using a potato peeler or a grater, grate shards of the remaining dark chocolate over the top of the cheesecake, before transferring it to the freezer to chill for at least 2 hours.

Serve frozen (or slightly defrosted if you prefer), topped with more whipped cream and a shot of Baileys on the side. To get the cheesecake out of the tin, run a sharp knife, dipped in boiling water, around the inside edge before unclipping the sides.

It should keep for 1 to 2 months in the freezer, wrapped in cling film.

—

TIP

For a non-alcoholic alternative, turn this into a Mint Aero cheesecake – one of my mum's favourites – by replacing the Baileys with two grated Mint Aero bars. Add the grated Aero to the mixture, holding some back to shave on top.

LEMON MERINGUE ICE CREAM

Lemon meringue is one of my favourite flavour combinations: pillowy, marshmallow-sweet meringue with lip-puckeringly bitter lemon curd. This quick-and-easy recipe transforms the popular pudding into an iced dessert, which is deliciously refreshing on a summer's day.

 SERVES 8–10

300ml double cream

300g Greek yoghurt

60g caster sugar

zest and juice of 1 lemon

40g meringues (either nests or miniature ones)

90g lemon curd

 PREP

Line a standard loaf tin (approx. 2lb or 1 litre) or freezer-proof Tupperware container with cling film, ensuring you cover the base and sides and leave plenty of excess overlapping the edges to cover the top. I use three strips — one for each long side and one for the middle. You'll also need an electric whisk, if you have one to hand.

 START THE CLOCK

Whisk the cream to soft peaks. As it's double cream it will thicken quickly, so this shouldn't take more than a minute or two.

In a separate bowl, mix together the yoghurt, sugar and lemon zest and juice. Gently fold this into the whipped cream, trying to retain as much air as possible in the mixture.

Crumble in the meringues, leaving reasonable-sized chunks, and mix thoroughly.

Transfer half the cream mixture to the loaf tin, and then drizzle on half the lemon curd, using a teaspoon to swirl it through. Tip the other half of the mixture into the tin and repeat with the remaining curd.

Wrap the cling film neatly over the top and freeze for at least 4 hours. Remove the ice cream from the freezer around 20 minutes before serving and use a sharp knife, dipped in warm water, to cut it into neat slices. Or you can scoop it, if you prefer.

Well covered, it should keep for 2 to 3 months in the freezer.

FREEZER BAG ICE CREAM

I first saw this magic trick at a birthday party when I was seven and it's stayed in my head ever since. Using nothing more than crushed ice and rock salt, you can transform liquid cream into soft-serve ice cream in an instant. This is a brilliant recipe to try with children: all that shaking and jiggling is great fun.

 SERVES 1

300ml single cream or coconut cream

45g caster sugar

½ tsp vanilla extract

400g crushed ice

250g rock salt

 PREP   You'll need two different sizes of freezer bag for this recipe: one small and another medium/large (big enough to comfortably fit the smaller one and all the ice inside). It's also useful to have a pair of oven gloves or an old tea towel to protect your hands from the c-c-c-cold!

 START THE CLOCK   Start by mixing the cream, sugar and vanilla extract together in a bowl and tip this into the small freezer bag. Seal it up and set to one side.

Put the crushed ice and rock salt into the larger freezer bag and shake it to make sure it's combined. Lower the ice cream bag inside, keeping the sealed end uppermost.

Now comes the magic part! Making sure the ice is in contact with the ice cream bag on all sides, start shaking, jiggling, pressing and generally squeezing the larger bag around the smaller one. Be careful not to break or pierce the bag.

You'll notice that the ice turns to water pretty quickly – don't worry, this is all down to the rock salt, which melts the ice and lowers the freezing point of the liquid left behind. Just keep going – after around 5 minutes you should notice the liquid in the small bag thickening up. Once it's all solidified, carefully remove the smaller bag, give it a quick rinse under the cold tap to remove the salt and decant the ice cream into a bowl.

Ta-daah! Six-minute freezer bag ice cream, whipped up before your eyes!

 TIP   *To turn this into raspberry ripple ice cream, add a tablespoon of jam or raspberry coulis to the bag in the final 20 seconds, or swirl it through the finished bowl. You could also try a spoonful of Nutella, a handful of chocolate chips, nuts or honeycomb pieces, or make freezer bag sorbet with a cup of fruit juice instead of cream.*

CINNAMON BUN BOMBE

This retro classic is so simple to whip up but looks utterly decadent. Made from sliced cinnamon buns, moulded to a bowl and filled with swirls of vanilla ice cream, salted caramel sauce and chunks of your favourite chocolate, it's a dreamy dessert guaranteed to impress.

**SERVES
8–10**

1500g cinnamon buns (approx. 5 large bakery ones or 2 packets of smaller ones), cut swirl-side up into 1cm thick slices – you'll need at least 15

100g white chocolate, broken into pieces

1 x 400g tub vanilla ice cream

100g shop-bought salted caramel sauce, plus extra for serving

100g of your favourite chocolate bar (I use Crunchies), chopped into chunks

PREP

Line a 1.5-litre Pyrex bowl (or any bowl will do as long as it's suitable for freezing) with overlapping strips of cling film, ensuring there's plenty of overhang around the sides. Not only will this help you take it out of the bowl, but it also covers the top and prevents freezer burn.

Take the ice cream out of the freezer around 15 minutes before you start so it's nice and soft. You'll also need a heatproof bowl for melting the chocolate.

**START
THE CLOCK**

Arrange the sliced cinnamon buns around the inside of the clingfilmed bowl. Start with one slice in the centre of the base and build a symmetrical pattern around it, filling the bowl almost to the top.

Squeeze the buns together to make sure there are no gaps for the ice cream to seep through. If you need to, slice some pieces up and use them to plug the holes.

Melt the white chocolate in the heatproof bowl in the microwave, heating on high for 20-second bursts (it shouldn't take longer than a minute). Or you can melt it over a pan of boiling water if you prefer. Use a spoon to spread it over the buns inside the main bowl. Make sure they are completely coated or the filling will seep out.

In a separate bowl, mix the soft ice cream, caramel sauce and chocolate chunks together until smooth. Tip this into the middle of the bombe; it should come almost to the top of the buns.

Gather together the excess cling film from around the edges of the bowl and draw it inwards, pressing everything together and completely covering the ice cream middle.

Freeze for at least 3 hours until the ice cream is solid again.

Invert the bombe, remove the cling film and serve it on a plate in the centre of the table, drizzled with yet more (hot) salted caramel sauce and chocolate chunks. Slice into tall, thin pieces.

You can refreeze any leftovers – they should keep for a couple of months in the freezer.

 TIP

If you can't find (or don't like) cinnamon buns, you can make this the traditional way instead, using slices of Swiss roll or chocolate log. You'll need two regular rolls (approx. 240g) for this recipe. Or you can use any sweet doughy bread: brioche, teacakes or even fruity malt loaf.

CHAPTER 9:

retro classics

Comforting, stodgy and utterly delicious,
this is the sort of baking your grandma would
approve of . . . made simpler and speedier

Coconut berry pavlova ◇ Rhubarb and custard trifle
◇ Sultana sponge ◇ Citrus surprise pud ◇ Gingerbread and butter pud
◇ Sticky toffee pots ◇ Easy cheesy soufflés ◇ Lemon syllabub
◇ Apple pie in a pan ◇ Chestnut creams

COCONUT BERRY PAVLOVA

My first book, *Three Ingredient Baking*, contains a recipe for microwave meringues. Little balls of icing sugar and egg white puff up like magic in the microwave to make fully formed meringues. This pavlova recipe goes one step further, using the same concept to make the perfect summer showstopper.

 SERVES 6

300g icing sugar

1 egg white

600g frozen mixed berries

300ml double cream

35g desiccated coconut

 PREP

Cut a circle of kitchen roll to around the same size as the rotating plate in your microwave. This is the base on which your pavlova will bake. You'll also need a hand whisk.

 START THE CLOCK

Sieve the icing sugar into a bowl and mix in the egg white. It should come together into a firm ball. Place this on the circle of kitchen roll in the microwave and flatten it slightly – not too much, as it will spread – to a diameter of no more than 8cm.

Microwave on high for 3 minutes. Watch it carefully; the sugar can burn quickly, so keep an eye on it while you get on with whisking the cream.

Take the berries out of the freezer. Tip the cream into a large bowl and whisk it by hand until it forms soft peaks – this shouldn't take more than a minute. Once it's at the right consistency, stir in 30g of the desiccated coconut and half the mixed berries.

Carefully slide the cooked pavlova base out of the microwave and on to your serving plate. Allow it to cool slightly before topping with the mixed berry cream and the rest of the frosted berries. Finish with the remaining 5g of coconut, scattered artfully over the top.

Serve at once: the microwaved meringue is brittle and won't keep well, so you have no option but it eat it all in one go!

 TIP

Pavlova is a very versatile recipe and you can try all sorts of combinations with the cream and fruit. Why not whip in some cocoa powder instead of coconut, or try topping with sliced apricots and honey or fresh mango, passion fruit and lime zest?

RHUBARB AND CUSTARD TRIFLE

Remember those rhubarb and custard boiled sweets you used to eat as a kid? This is a double-decker of a retro throwback, combining the flavours of my favourite penny sweets with trifle. There's quite a lot going on, so you'll need to keep your eye on the ball – but it's a lovely celebratory dessert. And you can make it alcoholic or not, depending on who's coming to tea.

30g flaked almonds

205g plain sponge or fairy cakes

2 x 560g tins of cooked stewed rhubarb

optional: 1 tbsp Madeira or sherry

50g caster sugar

1 litre shop-bought custard

50g stem ginger, drained and finely chopped

400ml double or whipping cream

PREP

I came up with this recipe as an excuse to use my new trifle dish – so you'll need one of those. Mine is a whopper, holding 3 litres. If yours is different in size, adjust the quantities accordingly. And if you don't have one, don't panic, you can use a large glass bowl instead.

Preheat the grill to high and prepare a baking sheet for toasting your almonds. Put two medium saucepans on a medium heat on the hob. And you'll need a whisk – electric, if you have one – and a piping bag or large sandwich bag.

START THE CLOCK

Spread the almonds out on the baking sheet and put them under the grill for 4 minutes to toast.

Crumble the sponge(s) into small pieces and arrange in the bottom of the trifle dish. Drain the tinned rhubarb, conserving 100ml of juice, and pour the juice over the sponge layer. If you're using it, add the tablespoon of Madeira/sherry now.

Tip the drained rhubarb into one of the saucepans and add the caster sugar. Pour the custard into the other pan and add the chopped ginger.

Stir both occasionally so they don't stick. The rhubarb should start to stew and caramelize, while the flavour of the ginger will infuse through the custard. Leave them for 3 minutes.

Meanwhile, whisk the cream to stiff peaks and decant it into a piping bag fitted with a large nozzle. If you don't have a piping bag, you can make your own by snipping one corner off a large sandwich bag to make a hole about 2cm in diameter.

Take both pans off the hob and take the almonds out of the oven. Now it's time to assemble your trifle.

Spoon the sweetened rhubarb over the sponge, followed by the ginger custard. Pipe the cream on top – you'll have to be quite delicate here, so it doesn't sink into the custard, but feel free to follow whatever pattern you fancy.

Finish by scattering the toasted almonds over the top.

Serve immediately, with a big spoon for dipping in. It looks fanciest on first serving, but there should be plenty for seconds and thirds. If you don't manage to eat it all, it'll keep in the fridge, well covered, for 3 to 4 days.

SULTANA SPONGE

Gorgeously warming and guaranteed to bring back memories of a grandparent who served you steamed puddings as a child, this fluffy sultana sponge is a retro classic. It doesn't need a ton of sugar because the juicy sultanas give it all the sweetness it needs.

 SERVES 6

100g unsalted butter, softened

200g plain flour

1 tsp baking powder

100g soft light brown sugar

100g sultanas (or raisins)

2 eggs

50ml semi-skimmed milk

 PREP

Grease and line a 20cm-round microwave-proof cake tin or 1-litre pudding basin. You'll also need some cling film to help the pudding steam as it cooks.

 START THE CLOCK

Mix the butter, flour and baking powder together until well combined. The mixture should look a little like breadcrumbs at this stage.

Stir in the sugar and sultanas.

Crack in the eggs, one at a time, stirring in between each. Finally, add the milk. You should end up with a wet, smooth batter.

Pour the batter into the prepared tin or bowl and spread it to the edges. Cover the dish with cling film and microwave it on high for 4 minutes.

Serve hot, with buckets of custard and (if you're feeling really indulgent) sticky caramel sauce. The cooked sponge can be kept in the fridge for 2 to 3 days – reheat as desired, 45 seconds on high per portion.

CITRUS SURPRISE PUD

Zesty with citrus fruit, this super-speedy sponge can be baked in an instant – and makes a delicious dessert. The steamed sponge is a retro classic, and this one comes with not one but two surprises: a hot, fruity layer on the base and a melted chocolate centre. Yum!

 SERVES 6

100g unsalted butter, softened	1 tsp vanilla extract
100g caster sugar	zest of an orange or a lemon
100g self-raising flour	100g lemon curd
2 eggs	100g white chocolate

 PREP

Grease a 1-litre pudding dish with a little butter. If you don't have one, an ordinary Pyrex bowl will do – or a small microwaveable cake tin. You'll also need an electric whisk.

START THE CLOCK

In a large bowl, cream together the butter and sugar with the whisk until pale and fluffy.

Sieve in the flour and add the eggs, vanilla extract and fruit zest. Mix well to combine into a smooth batter.

Spoon the fruit curd into the base of the prepared pudding bowl and top with half the batter. Lay the chocolate pieces over this and top with the remaining batter.

Place the bowl on a microwave-proof plate (in case of spillage) and heat the pudding on high for 4 minutes, until it's baked and risen.

Leave the pud to cool for a minute or so before tipping it up on to a large serving plate. Carefully – using a tea towel or oven gloves – lift the pudding bowl off the sponge.

Use a knife to spread the curd neatly over the top and down the sides. Serve steaming hot, with ice cream or warm custard.

If you don't eat it all in one go, it can be kept in the fridge for 2 to 3 days and reheated (1 minute in the microwave per portion) as required.

 TIP

If white chocolate and lemon isn't for you, try switching them for dark chocolate and orange marmalade – the recipe works just the same!

GINGERBREAD AND BUTTER PUD

This comforting dessert combines two of my great loves: bread and butter pudding and Jamaican ginger loaf. Rich, spiced and studded with tasty morsels, it's guaranteed to brighten up even the gloomiest of days and warm you up from the inside out.

 SERVES 6–8

2 x 232g ginger loaves, cut into 1cm slices

100g dark chocolate, chopped into chunks

100g stem ginger, drained and finely chopped

50g chopped pecan nuts

50ml milk (I use semi-skimmed as a nod to being healthy)

75ml double cream

1 tbsp unsalted butter, melted, plus extra for greasing

40g golden caster sugar

2 eggs

 PREP

Preheat the grill to high. Grease a large rectangular Pyrex dish (mine is around 20cm x 30cm, microwave- and ovenproof) with a little butter or flavourless oil. You'll also need a whisk.

 START THE CLOCK

Lay the slices of ginger cake in whatever pattern you like, but partially overlapping, across the base of the dish.

Scatter over the various toppings: chocolate, stem ginger and pecans.

Whisk together the milk, cream, butter, sugar and eggs and pour this over the top of the buttered bread, making sure it's evenly distributed but leaving a few corners poking out the top (these will crisp up nicely in the oven).

Microwave the pudding for 3 minutes on high, and then place it on the top shelf of the grill for another minute. Keep an eye on it as the chocolate can catch and burn quickly. Switch the grill off and leave the pudding inside to keep warm until you're ready to serve.

It will keep for 4 to 5 days in the fridge and can be microwaved to reheat, either all at once or a portion at a time.

STICKY TOFFEE POTS

This section wouldn't be complete without an ode to the sticky toffee pudding – the ultimate in homely, gooey stodge. These little date-studded sponge pots taste just like the pud that takes hours to rustle up, but they're baked in the microwave – giving you enough time to make that sauce.

 MAKES 2 LARGE POTS (4 IF USING SMALLER DISHES)

90g plain flour

½ tsp baking powder

30ml double cream

2 tbsp golden syrup (or molasses or treacle)

1 egg

½ tsp vanilla extract

a pinch of salt

100g soft pitted dates or prunes, finely chopped

For the toffee sauce:

90g unsalted butter

80g soft dark brown sugar

2 tbsp water

 PREP

Prep your pots: I use two 175ml ramekins, but if yours are bigger or smaller then plan your portions accordingly. There's plenty of sauce here for four, so don't worry! Grease them with a little butter.

Place a small saucepan over a medium-high heat on the hob.

START THE CLOCK

Put the sauce ingredients in the saucepan, mix to combine and leave these to simmer away while you make the puddings.

Mix together all the sponge ingredients, except the dates, and beat until you have a smooth batter. Add in the chopped dates and stir to combine.

Divide the pudding batter between your pots and microwave on high for 4 minutes. You'll know they're done when the sponge is risen and springs back to the touch.

Meanwhile, keep stirring your toffee sauce. As it cooks, it will bubble and thicken – it needs about 4 to 5 minutes in total. Keep an eye on it so it doesn't stick or burn, and if you want it thinner, just add another teaspoon of water.

Once the sauce is at your desired thickness, take it off the heat. Tip the puddings out on to plates and cover completely with generous portions of toffee sauce. Eat immediately!

EASY CHEESY SOUFFLÉS

Soufflés are notoriously difficult to get right: too little air and they're flat as pancakes, too much and they'll sink like deflating balloons before they reach the table. Mine contain a smidge of cream of tartar, a slightly acidic salt that acts as a stabilizer, so they're guaranteed not to collapse.

 MAKES 2

25g salted butter

2 eggs

25g plain flour

1 tsp cream of tartar

a pinch of salt and a good grind of black pepper

120ml milk (I use semi-skimmed)

75g hard cheese (such as Cheddar, Parmesan or Gruyère), finely grated

a handful of chopped chives

 PREP

Grease two microwaveable mugs (approx. 300ml capacity) with a little butter or flavourless oil. Cut strips of greaseproof paper – around 5cm wide and 12cm long – and stick them around the inside rims of the mugs, so the paper forms a 'crown' that sticks out of the top.

An electric whisk will come in handy, but a hand whisk will do.

 START THE CLOCK

Melt the butter in a pan. Separate the eggs and whisk the whites to soft peaks while the butter melts. Give the yolks a quick stir with a fork to break them up.

Take the butter off the heat and stir in the flour, cream of tartar and seasoning, followed by the egg yolks and the milk, whisking constantly so there are no lumps.

Using a large metal spoon, fold in the egg whites, taking care to retain as much air in the mixture as possible. Finally, stir in all but a small handful of cheese.

Sprinkle the remaining cheese into the base of each mug and top with the soufflé mix, divided evenly between them. Microwave on high for 2.5 to 3 minutes, until puffed up and spongey.

Carefully remove the greaseproof paper 'crowns' from each mug and eat the soufflés hot, straight from the mugs, topped with chopped chives and some more black pepper.

LEMON SYLLABUB

A syllabub is an old English dessert that dates back to the sixteenth century. Made from milk or cream, plus wine or cider, it was popular at banquets and celebrations. My sweet-and-sour lemon version makes a lovely after-dinner palate-cleanser. The addition of wine (or a non-alcoholic alternative) cuts through the cream and gives it the most incredible velvety texture.

 MAKES 2

300ml double or whipping cream

60g golden caster sugar

60ml white wine (or grape juice if you prefer)

zest and juice of 1 lemon

80g lemon curd

3 digestive biscuits, crushed

 PREP

You'll need two serving bowls or glasses — I use 200ml tumblers — and be generous, as you'll want a big helping. There's a lot of whisking, so an electric whisk will also come in handy.

—

 START THE CLOCK

Whisk the cream and sugar together until the mixture reaches the consistency of soft peaks.

Add the white wine, lemon zest and juice and whisk again. The mixture will be thinner, but you should still be able to get it nice and airy.

Divide the syllabub between the two serving bowls or glasses, spooning it in carefully so it doesn't go all over the glass. Smooth down the top.

Spoon a thin layer of lemon curd over each and spread it out so it covers the syllabub entirely. Top with biscuit crumbs.

Serve immediately, or chilled if you prefer. The syllabubs will keep for 2 to 3 days in the fridge.

APPLE PIE IN A PAN

Stodgy, autumnal and packed full of juicy fruit and crunchy crumbly topping . . . it's hard to beat an old-fashioned apple pie. My version is a sort of thrown-together cobbler, mixing all the best bits in a single batter that cooks in a frying pan like a pancake. You can put the pan in the centre of the table, topped with clotted cream or served with a jug of hot custard.

 SERVES 6–8

4 apples (approx. 375g), peeled, cored and chopped into small chunks

200g rolled oats

200g crunchy peanut butter

2 eggs

100g caster sugar

a pinch of cinnamon, mixed spice or nutmeg

 PREP

Heat a knob of butter in a large, heavy-based frying pan (with a lid) over a high heat.

—

 START THE CLOCK

Mix all the ingredients together in a bowl until well combined.

Tip the mixture into the pan and flatten it down using a wooden spoon. Put the lid on and allow it to cook for 2 minutes on one side.

Using a dinner plate to cover the 'pie', tip the pan upside down so that the contents fall on to the plate, then slide the pie back into the pan to cook the other way up. Allow it to cook for another 2 minutes before serving hot.

You can keep this, well covered, in the fridge for 2 to 3 days, but it's best eaten on the day it's made.

 TIP

—

This works with all sorts of delicious seasonal fruit, so try it with blackberries, pears, rhubarb or gooseberries – whatever you have to hand.

CHESTNUT CREAMS

The nutty sweetness of chestnuts – roasted (on an open fire, obviously) and then puréed – really comes through in this simple but stunning recipe. By adding a little sugar, chocolate and cream to chestnut purée, you can transform these humble nuts into something miraculous.

 MAKES 4 POTS

200g unsweetened chestnut purée (you can buy this in pouches or jars from supermarkets)

100g caster sugar

100g dark chocolate

200ml double or whipping cream

1 tsp cocoa powder

 PREP

Clean and dry four small ramekins, pots or glasses (mine can hold approx. 175ml – so make sure you have more/fewer to hand if yours are very different in size).

Put a small saucepan on the hob over a medium heat. You'll also need a whisk, and a cocktail stick might be useful for swirling.

 START THE CLOCK

Put the chestnut purée, sugar and chocolate in the pan and heat gently, stirring occasionally to stop it sticking to the bottom. It should melt and come together into a smooth, thick liquid – give it approximately 3 to 4 minutes.

While this cooks, whisk the cream to soft peaks.

If there are any lumps left in the chestnut mixture, run it through a sieve until it's nice and smooth. Fold in the cream, a spoonful at a time. Hold back a tablespoon of unmixed cream for swirling through the tops of the pots.

Divide the mixture evenly between the serving dishes. Use the remaining cream – and a cocktail stick if this helps – to swirl a little circle on the top of each. Finish with a sprinkling of cocoa powder.

Put the pots in the fridge and leave them for around 2 hours to set. You can eat them straight away if you prefer – they'll still be delicious, just quite runny.

They'll keep for 3 to 4 days in the fridge.

CHAPTER 10:

sweets and chocolates

Ferrero Rocher fudge, gingerbread truffles,

unicorn bark and buried treasure tiffin . . .

these treats will satisfy your sweet-tooth cravings

Unicorn bark ◇ Brown butter krispie shards ◇ Coconut snowballs
◇ Sticky gingerbread truffles ◇ Carrot cake bites ◇ Maple pecan fudge
◇ Buried treasure tiffin ◇ Salted date caramels ◇ Ferrero Rocher fudge
◇ Christmas pud petit fours ◇ Mississippi mud shots

UNICORN BARK

Unicorns – or at least unicorn-inspired rainbow colours, glitter and sparkle – are everywhere you look these days, from cakes to cushion covers, croissants to cocktails. I've taken a simple recipe for chocolate bark and given it a fairytale twist – guaranteed to put a smile on people's faces.

**MAKES
15–20
PIECES**

600g white chocolate

1 tsp coconut oil

at least 3 vivid gel food colourings (I use purple, blue and pink super-strength gels by Dr Oetker)

whatever toppings take your fancy: e.g. mini marshmallows, rainbow sprinkles, silver balls

 PREP

Line a large chopping board with greaseproof paper. It also makes life easier if you prepare your food colouring stations in advance, so lay out three small bowls and teaspoons. Have a ladle and palette knife to hand too, and a large Pyrex bowl for melting the chocolate.

—

 START THE CLOCK

Put the chocolate and coconut oil in the Pyrex bowl and microwave on high for 1 to 1.5 minutes until melted (you can do this in shorter bursts if you want, or you can suspend the bowl over a pan of boiling water). Give the mixture a good stir to get rid of any lumps.

Using the ladle, transfer around a sixth of the melted chocolate mixture to each of the smaller bowls, ensuring you leave around half in the main bowl.

Squeeze out a teaspoonful of food dye into each of the three bowls and stir until the colour is strong and evenly distributed.

Start assembling the bark. First, tip the undyed white chocolate on to the prepared board and use the palette knife to spread it out. Next, drizzle over each of the coloured chocolate mixtures in turn, using the spoon to marble them through the white chocolate.

Top with marshmallows, sprinkles and anything else that takes your fancy. Transfer to a cool place or the fridge for at least an hour to harden, before breaking up into pieces.

The bark will keep for up to a week in an airtight tin, and makes a lovely present or after dinner treat – whether you're 3 or 93!

—

 TIP

Don't feel you have to stick to unicorn-style bark. You can experiment with all sorts of flavour and colour combinations, such as dark chocolate with pistachios (35g) and cranberries (75g), white chocolate with dried strawberries (100g) and black pepper, milk chocolate with crunchy peanut butter (100g) and sea salt, or how about milk chocolate with salted pretzels (35g) and boiled sweets (35g)?

BROWN BUTTER KRISPIE SHARDS

When I was little, Rice Krispie squares were the highlight of any birthday party – and when they started selling them in packs at the supermarket, I could barely contain myself (as an adult). These brown butter shards are the grown-up version: salty, a little bit sharp – and perfect as an after-dinner treat, served with a strong espresso.

MAKES 8–10 LARGE SHARDS

50g Rice Krispies

75g salted butter

100g white marshmallows, roughly chopped

80g dark chocolate, broken into pieces

a generous pinch of sea salt

 PREP

Put a large frying pan and a medium saucepan on the hob and turn the heat up high. Line a baking sheet or chopping board with greaseproof paper, rubbed with a little butter (this will stop the shards from sticking once they set). You'll also need a spare sheet of greaseproof, a rolling pin and a Pyrex bowl for melting the chocolate.

 START THE CLOCK

Tip the Rice Krispies into the frying pan and the butter into the saucepan. You want the cereal to lightly brown and the butter to melt and then brown a little. This gives it a deep, almost malty flavour. Keep an eye on both – they can turn quickly, so keep stirring.

Take the toasted Krispies off the heat. When the butter has browned (it should only take a minute or two), add the marshmallows to the pan and stir until they melt.

Pour the Krispies into the saucepan and stir to combine. Tip the mixture out on to the prepared baking sheet and, working quickly, place the spare sheet of greaseproof paper on top. Use the rolling pin to flatten the mixture until it's thin (no more than half a centimetre thick).

Melt the chocolate in the Pyrex bowl – either in 20-second bursts on high in the microwave or suspended over a saucepan of boiling water. Drizzle this over the flattened cereal mix (you can be as artistic as you like) and sprinkle with sea salt.

Allow it to cool in the fridge for an hour (or in the freezer for 20 minutes if you're in a hurry) before breaking up into long, thin shards.

Keep them in an airtight tin and they'll stay crisp for 2 to 3 days.

COCONUT SNOWBALLS

My brother has a soft spot for coconut, so these are for him. Fluffy, sweet and melt-in-the-mouth delicious, these bite-sized balls will transport you from your kitchen to a sun-drenched tropical island, where palm trees sway in the breeze.

MAKES ABOUT 12

175g desiccated coconut

3 tsp coconut oil, slightly warmed so it's liquid

a pinch of sea salt

3 tbsp coconut milk (any milk will do, but this will make

the coconut flavour even more intense)

3 tbsp maple syrup or honey

½ tsp vanilla extract

½ tsp ground cinnamon

PREP

Put 25g desiccated coconut into a bowl for dipping the snowballs. Cover a small plate with greaseproof paper to set them on. You'll also need a food processor.

START THE CLOCK

Put 150g desiccated coconut, along with the coconut oil and sea salt, into the food processor and blitz on high speed for 30 seconds.

Add the rest of the ingredients and blend until the mixture starts coming together into a ball.

Tip it out into a bowl and, using clean but slightly damp palms, pick up blobs of the mix – around the size of a 50p piece – and roll them between your palms.

Roll each one in the remaining coconut before placing on the plate. Once you've used up all the mix, put the plate in the fridge for around an hour to chill (you can eat the snowballs straight away but they're quite crumbly, so are best left to firm up a little).

They'll keep for 4 to 5 days in an airtight container (and a few days longer in the fridge).

STICKY GINGERBREAD TRUFFLES

These sticky, stodgy treats make me feel all wintery. The heady, aromatic flavour of gingerbread inside a nutty chocolate truffle, drizzled with melted dark chocolate . . . it's a mouthful of magic. To make a healthier version, you could use maple syrup or honey instead of golden syrup, but for me these truffles are all about indulgence.

**MAKES
12–14**

150g soft pitted dates (I use Medjool – available from most supermarkets – as they're extra juicy)

80g pecan nuts

25g cocoa powder

1 tsp ground ginger (plus a pinch for dusting)

½ tsp ground cinnamon

½ tsp ground nutmeg

2 tbsp golden syrup

100g dark chocolate, broken into pieces

½ tsp coconut oil (to give them a lovely professional sheen)

 PREP

To properly purée the dates, you'll need a food processor, blender or hand blender, and you'll need a Pyrex bowl for melting the chocolate. Prepare a small board or side plate for chilling the truffles.

 **START
THE CLOCK**

Put the dates in the food processor and blitz until smooth. Scrape down the sides, using a knife if they start to get stuck: you want to get rid of all the lumps.

Add the pecans, cocoa powder, spices and golden syrup and pulse again until the mixture comes together into a sticky ball.

Tip this out into a bowl and, using damp hands, take handfuls of the mix and roll it into balls, each around the size of a 50p piece.

Put the chocolate in the Pyrex bowl with the coconut oil and melt it by heating it on high in the microwave for 20-second bursts (it should take around a minute), or you can put the bowl over a pan of boiling water. Use a teaspoon to drizzle the chocolate artfully over the tops of the truffles.

Finally, top each truffle with a sprinkle of ground ginger and decorate as desired.

Pop them in the fridge to chill. They'll stay fresh for around 4 to 5 days – either chilled or in an airtight container.

CARROT CAKE BITES

Sweet, nutty and aromatic from all those spices, these little morsels have all the flavour of carrot cake in a tasty bite-sized mouthful. A cross between a protein ball and a truffle, they're even a little bit healthy – so you can eat as many as you want, guilt-free.

MAKES ABOUT 20

130g pitted dates

1 large carrot (approx. 90g), peeled and chopped

200g ground almonds

½ tsp mixed spice

1 tbsp golden syrup

1½ tsp ground cinnamon

1 tbsp icing sugar, sifted

 PREP

This recipe works best if you have a food processor, blender or hand blender, so you can purée the dates. Place a side plate or a small board in the fridge for chilling the bites later.

—

 START THE CLOCK

Put the dates in the food processor and blitz until they're nice and soft (they may start to come together into a ball, so use a knife to scrape down the sides if you need to).

Add the chopped carrot and repeat. Finally, add the ground almonds, mixed spice, syrup and 1 tsp cinnamon.

When the mixture has come together, tip it into a bowl and give it a final stir to make sure there are no lumps.

Take handfuls of the mix and roll it into small balls, roughly the size of 50p pieces. There should be enough to make around 20.

In a small bowl, mix the icing sugar with the remaining cinnamon and dust over the top of the bites to finish. Put them in the fridge to chill before eating – they should last for 4 to 5 days.

—

 TIP

If you have a sticky mixture, it's easiest to roll truffles, balls or bites using slightly wet hands. This stops the mixture from attaching itself to your palms and will give a smoother, rounder ball shape. Simply rinse your hands under a running tap and don't dry them off before starting.

MAPLE PECAN FUDGE

For me, rich maple and toasted pecans are the very essence of autumnal flavours – and I can think of nothing I'd rather tuck into as the leaves start turning brown than this moreish fudge. The salted butter and maple flavour balance the sweetness, while the nuts add crunch to every bite.

 MAKES 36 SQUARES

400g white chocolate, broken into pieces

1 x 397g tin of condensed milk

50g salted butter

120g pecan nuts, chopped

3 tbsp maple syrup

 PREP

Line a small square tin (mine is 20cm x 20cm) with tin foil, ensuring you press it right into the corners so the fudge will have neat edges.

Preheat the grill to high and prepare a baking sheet to toast the pecans. You'll also need a large Pyrex bowl for melting the chocolate.

 START THE CLOCK

Put the chocolate in the Pyrex bowl and microwave on high for 1 minute, by which stage it should have started to melt. (You can do the melting over a pan of boiling water, if you prefer.)

Add the butter and condensed milk, using a spatula to scrape out every last drop from the tin, and microwave on high for another 1.5 minutes.

While this cooks, spread the chopped pecans over a baking tray and put them under the grill for a few minutes – but keep an eye on them as they'll burn quickly. When they're brown and toasty, take them out to cool.

Stir the bowl of melted ingredients and add 1 tablespoon of the maple syrup, followed by all but a handful of nuts. Mix thoroughly.

Using the spatula again, transfer the fudge mixture to the prepared baking tin, spreading it evenly over the base. Top with the remaining nuts and drizzle over the rest of the maple syrup, using a knife to create a marbled pattern on the top.

Put the tray in the fridge for 3 to 4 hours to set, before cutting into small squares. They will keep in an airtight tin for 4 or 5 days.

 TIP

This works well with any type of nuts – hazelnuts, almonds, macadamia nuts or walnuts – not just pecans. Just chop and toast them in the same way.

BURIED TREASURE TIFFIN

I love tiffin: chocolatey, buttery, syrupy, biscuity . . . it's the ultimate indulgent snack. But I was getting a bit bored of those chunks of shortbread, raisins and nuts that popped up in every recipe. So here's my pimped-up version: a showstopping tiffin containing a treasure trove of colourful, tasty treats, enrobed in marbled chocolate. Kids – both big and small – will have a field day.

 MAKES 32 SQUARES

200g milk chocolate

200g dark chocolate

270g unsalted butter

3 tbsp golden syrup

200g digestive biscuits

100g white chocolate

For the buried treasure (you can use all or some of the following):

2 Bounty bars (57g each), chopped into chunks

2 packets of Smarties (38g each)

100g Maltesers or chunks of Toblerone, chopped up

a handful of: mini marshmallows, raisins, a handful of nuts of your choice, broken-up pretzels

 PREP

Line a large rectangular baking tin (approx. 20cm x 30cm) with tin foil, pressing it neatly into the corners and edges. You'll also need one large and two smaller Pyrex bowls for melting the chocolate and a food processor (or a ziplock bag and a rolling pin) for crushing the biscuits.

 START THE CLOCK

Put the milk chocolate, 100g dark chocolate, butter and syrup into the large Pyrex bowl and microwave on high for 1 to 1.5 minutes, stirring halfway, until it's all melted together (or you can suspend it over a pan of boiling water if you prefer).

While this melts, crush the digestives in the food processor (or put them into a ziplock bag and bash them with a rolling pin). You want them to turn to tiny crumbs, so keep going until there are no chunks left.

Put the biscuit crumbs into a large bowl and pour over the chocolate mixture. Stir until combined.

Now it's time for the treasure. Stir everything together, working quickly so the chocolatey bits don't melt too much, and tip it into the prepared tin, pressing it down so it's nice and compact.

Next, melt the remaining dark chocolate and the white chocolate, in separate bowls, on high in the microwave. Do it in bursts of 20 seconds so they don't burn or go grainy.

Drizzle the two colours of melted chocolate over the tiffin, marbling them across the top. You can do this freehand as you pour, or use a knife or cocktail stick if you prefer.

Put the tiffin in the fridge for a few hours to harden, before slicing it into squares. It will keep for 3 to 4 days in an airtight tin, or a few days longer in the fridge.

SALTED DATE CARAMELS

If you love caramel but are looking for something a liiiittle bit healthier, this is the recipe for you. Puréed dates, when combined with sea salt, make the most delicious salted caramel, packed full of natural sugars, which will satisfy the fussiest of caramel connoisseurs.

 MAKES
14

250g soft pitted dates

1 tsp sea salt

150g dark chocolate

 PREP

Give the dates a squeeze to check how juicy they are. If they feel a little dry (as many supermarket brands tend to be), stick them in a bowl covered with boiling water and soak them for 10 minutes to give a nice sticky consistency.

Prepare a large dinner plate or chopping board by covering it with some greaseproof paper. You'll also need a food processor and a Pyrex bowl for melting the chocolate.

—

 START
THE CLOCK

Blitz the dates in the food processor with most of the salt. Keep pulsing until it reaches the consistency of thick peanut butter. If it's still a little dry (and it won't be if you've soaked your dates first), add a teaspoon at a time of boiling water until you get the right texture.

While the dates are puréeing, melt the chocolate in the Pyrex bowl – either in 20-second bursts on high in the microwave or over a pan of boiling water on the hob – and set it aside to cool.

Tip the salted caramel date mix out into a bowl and, using wet hands, roll it into small balls (around the size of 50p pieces).

In turn, and using a fork or spoon if you need to, dunk the balls in the cooled melted chocolate, roll them around so they're completely covered, and transfer them to the greaseproof-covered plate or board.

Sprinkle the caramels with a little more sea salt and then put them somewhere cool (in the fridge or a cold corner of the kitchen) to set.

They should keep for 4 to 5 days, and will last best if you keep them in the fridge.

FERRERO ROCHER FUDGE

With all the crunch, smooth creaminess and delicious nutty flavour of Ferrero Rocher, my speedy fudge wouldn't look out of place on the Ambassador's dining table! It sets quickly, so you don't have to wait long before tucking in – and it makes a great celebratory gift for friends or family.

 MAKES 36 SQUARES

200g Nutella (or any other brand of chocolate spread)

300g dark chocolate

1 x 397g tin of condensed milk

25g unsalted butter

8 Ferrero Rocher (approx. 100g)

50g icing sugar

 PREP

Line a small square baking tin (mine is 20cm x 20cm) with tin foil, pressing it right into the corners and edges. Put a heavy-bottomed saucepan over a medium heat (or use a large Pyrex bowl and the microwave).

 START THE CLOCK

Put the Nutella, chocolate, condensed milk and butter in the saucepan and stir together for 3 to 4 minutes until the mixture is melted and smooth. (If you're microwaving, melt the mixture on high in bursts of 20 seconds, giving it a stir between each burst.)

Meanwhile, chop the Ferrero Rocher into chunks. You can crumble them with your fingers if you prefer, but beware – it's messy. Scatter half the chocolates over the base of the prepared tin.

When the fudge mixture is smooth, take it off the heat and sieve in the icing sugar. Stir until it's all well combined.

Pour the fudge over the top of the Ferrero Rocher in the tin, making sure you scrape every bit out of the pan. Scatter the remaining chocolate pieces over the top and press down.

Put it in the fridge or set aside in a cool place to set for around 3 hours. When it's hard, use a sharp knife to chop it into squares. The fudge will keep for up to 5 days in an airtight tin.

CHRISTMAS PUD PETIT FOURS

These bite-sized festive treats are ridiculously easy to make and require just five ingredients – so there's no excuse not to give them a go. The decoration may sound fiddly, but follow the steps below and you'll be a pro in no time. Serve them after a meal, with coffee, as a posh petit four.

MAKES AROUND 20

300g Christmas pudding, cooked and cooled

75g dark chocolate, melted

½ tsp ground nutmeg

90g white chocolate, melted

Red and green sprinkles (or use jelly diamonds, which you can cut into the shapes of leaves and berries)

 PREP

For added festive sparkle, I like to put these in gold or silver petit four cases – or you can serve them on a pretty platter. You'll also need a cocktail stick or skewer for the decoration.

 START THE CLOCK

Break the Christmas pudding up in a bowl and add the melted dark chocolate and nutmeg. Stir until it's well combined and comes together in a sticky ball.

Wet your hands and roll small blobs of the mix (around the size of 50p pieces) between your palms. Place them in the petit four cases or on your serving platter.

Drizzle small teaspoonfuls of melted white chocolate over the top of each – this serves as the 'brandy butter' on your miniature Christmas puddings. Use a cocktail stick or skewer to drag small 'drips' of the white chocolate at intervals down the sides of the balls.

Arrange the coloured sprinkles to look like holly berries and leaves on the tops of your puds.

Put the petit fours in the fridge to set before serving. They'll keep for 4 to 5 days – if your kitchen is hot it's best to keep them chilled so the white chocolate doesn't melt.

 TIP

If you're not feeling festive, or fancy making these in the middle of July, you can use ordinary fruit cake in place of Christmas pudding – or any other heavy, moist sponge (such as leftover carrot cake, coffee and walnut cake or ginger cake) – and decorate accordingly.

Also, bear in mind that Christmas pud can be microwaved – just check the back of the packet – so you don't have to slave for hours over a steamer.

MISSISSIPPI MUD SHOTS

As a child, I was obsessed with Mississippi mud pie. But even I, a seasoned chocaholic, could never manage to eat an entire slice. These little after-dinner treats are miniature versions (sort of), made with that retro classic, Angel Delight – and can be adapted for kids or adults, depending on your audience.

MAKES 6

50g milk chocolate, melted

50g white chocolate, melted

½ a pack of instant chocolate whipped pudding (30g)

150ml semi-skimmed milk (if you're making this for grown-ups, you can swap a third of this for a cream-based liqueur, such as Baileys or Kahlúa)

100ml double or whipping cream

6 Oreo biscuits (approx. 65g), crumbled

PREP

The key to making these little mud shots is the chocolate moulds. You'll need six cupcake moulds – silicone is best as they're really easy to flip inside out and peel off without cracking the chocolate. If you don't have any, you can use disposable plastic/paper cups or cases instead, but this will make the process a little fiddly.

You'll also need a hand whisk, and a small paintbrush or pastry brush.

—

START THE CLOCK

Put a teaspoon of both melted white and milk chocolate in each of the silicone cases. Using the paintbrush or pastry brush, swirl the chocolate around the base and brush it up the sides until it reaches the top of the case. If you're using cups instead, go about halfway up.

Try to make the chocolate layer even and relatively thick; don't let it all drip down into the bottom. And keep the marbled effect as much as possible. Transfer the cases to the freezer for 5 minutes.

While the chocolate sets, make up the chocolate pudding by whisking the powder with the milk (and liqueur, if you're using it) until frothy. Set this aside to thicken.

In a separate bowl, whisk the cream to soft peaks. Fold this into the thickened pudding mix and crumble in the biscuits, holding back a few teaspoonfuls.

Take the chocolate-lined cases out of the freezer and fill with the chocolate pudding mix, piling it nice and high. Crumble the remaining biscuit pieces over the top.

Put the mud shots in the fridge to chill until needed. They'll keep for 2 to 3 days in the fridge. You can keep the chocolate cases, unfilled, in the freezer for up to a week.

TIP

—

Try making this with different biscuits (Bourbons or Hobnobs work well), different types of chocolate (such as dark and white) or different flavours of Angel Delight – I've experimented with strawberry and butterscotch.

ACKNOWLEDGEMENTS

This book would not exist without an awful lot of help and support (and some seriously big appetites) from an awful lot of people. So, in no particular order, I'd like to thank . . .

The brilliant team at Michael Joseph, without whom this whole project would be a figment of my imagination. I never dreamed I would have a cookery book with my name on it, let alone a second, so thank you from the bottom of my heart for your encouragement, for your faith in me, and for bringing my little idea out into the world with such pizzazz. Special thanks to: Ione Walder, editor extraordinaire; fellow Starbar appreciator Amy McWalters; Sarah Fraser, Daniel Bunyard, Sriya Varadharajan, Emma Henderson and everyone else behind the scenes who made it happen.

Emma Lahaye, possibly the world's greatest home economist / props stylist / superwoman, for making my showstoppers look so, well, showstopping. Your boundless energy and culinary wizardry put us all to shame. And Octavia Squire, for your brilliance in the kitchen and the ready supply of Charlie cuddles on set.

Clare Winfield, for your stunning photographs, the endless cups of tea, and just for being so utterly lovely. You are one of life's good people and I hope we get to work together again.

Others to whom I owe a debt of thanks: my superstar agent Clare Hulton; my colleagues and editors at the *Mail*, especially Celia Duncan, for letting me share my recipe ideas in a weekly column; eagle-eyed copy-editor Emma Horton; the Hilton family, my lovely friends, and all the people who subscribe to my website or follow me on Instagram or Twitter, who have been so generous in their comments and reviews. Your support is truly humbling.

My wonderful family – Mum, Dad, Anna and David – for bringing me up to love food: cooking it, eating it, experimenting with it, and, of course, feeding it to others. Mum, thank you for teaching me to bake, and for passing on all that passion that your mum instilled in you. Grandma's scones will always make my heart sing. Thank you all for eating my weird and wonderful creations over the years, for your endless enthusiasm and honest feedback, for spreading the word about my baking, and for generally being the best family around. Raineys rule.

Mikey, my husband, best friend, chief taster, domestic god. Thank you for letting me devote evenings and weekends to recipe-testing, for tasting everything I put in front of you, and for not complaining (too much) when you had to re-clean the kitchen after I caused havoc with the icing sugar / flour / chocolate / hundreds and thousands (delete as appropriate). You are my sounding board, my rock, and forever on my team. Especially now that we're a three!

And finally – littlest but never least – my Charlie Bear. You were growing in my tummy while I wrote and tested these recipes. You are my greatest inspiration, my favourite person in the universe – and the reason there is so much sweet stuff in these pages! Pregnancy cravings have a lot to answer for. Namely the copious amounts of Nutella and cheese. I hope that, one day, we can bake from these pages together. But don't grow up too fast; I'm already the proudest mummy in the world.

INDEX

MICHAEL JOSEPH

UK | USA | Canada | Ireland | Australia
India | New Zealand | South Africa

Michael Joseph is part of the Penguin Random House group of companies
whose addresses can be found at global.penguinrandomhouse.com.

First published 2020
001

Copyright © Sarah Rainey, 2020
Photography copyright © Clare Winfield, 2020

The moral right of the author has been asserted

Set in Agenda, Caslon Graphique, Futura Maxi Std, Placard MT, ITC Century Book
Colour reproduction by Altaimage Ltd
Printed in China by RR Donnelley

A CIP catalogue record for this book is available from the British Library

ISBN: 978-0-241-37921-9

www.greenpenguin.co.uk